First World War
and Army of Occupation
War Diary
France, Belgium and Germany

46 DIVISION
137 Infantry Brigade,
Brigade Machine Gun Company
25 February 1916 - 14 February 1918

WO95/2687/2

The Naval & Military Press Ltd
www.nmarchive.com
Published in association with The National Archives

Published by

The Naval & Military Press Ltd

Unit 10 Ridgewood Industrial Park,

Uckfield, East Sussex,

TN22 5QE England

Tel: +44 (0) 1825 749494

www.naval-military-press.com

www.nmarchive.com

This diary has been reprinted in facsimile from the original. Any imperfections are inevitably reproduced and the quality may fall short of modern type and cartographic standards.

© **Crown Copyright**
Images reproduced by permission of The National Archives, London, England, 2015.

Contents

Document type	Place/Title	Date From	Date To
Heading	WO95/2687/2 Brigade Machine Gun Company		
Heading	46th Division 137th Infy Bde 137th Machine Gun Coy. Feb 1916-Feb 1918		
War Diary	Les Mazures	25/02/1916	07/03/1916
War Diary	Les Mazures	01/03/1916	11/05/1916
War Diary	Fonquevillers	18/05/1916	02/07/1916
War Diary	Berles Au Bois	03/07/1916	31/07/1916
Heading	War Diary of 137th Machine Gun Company For The Month Of August 1916 Vol 7		
War Diary	Berles au Bois.	01/08/1916	14/08/1916
War Diary	Berles	15/08/1916	31/08/1916
War Diary	Berles Au Bois	00/08/1916	00/08/1916
Diagram etc	Machine Gun Coy.		
Heading	War Diary of 137th Trench Mortar Battery From 1st August 1916 to 31st August 1916 Vol 4		
Miscellaneous	137 Field Mortar Battery	20/08/1917	20/08/1917
War Diary	In The Field.	01/08/1916	31/08/1916
Heading	War Diary of 137th Machine Gun Company. From 1st September 1916. To 30th September 1916 Vol 8		
War Diary	Berles	01/09/1916	30/09/1916
Heading	War Diary of 137th Machine Gun Coy Date 1st Oct 1916 To 31st Oct 1916		
War Diary	Berles.	01/10/1916	30/10/1916
War Diary	Brevillers.	31/10/1916	01/11/1916
War Diary	Fortel.	02/11/1916	03/11/1916
War Diary	Hanchy	04/11/1916	30/11/1916
War Diary	Brevillers.	01/12/1916	04/12/1916
War Diary	Map Ref Ransart 57 C S.E & Fonquevillers 57 D.N.E 1/10,000	04/12/1916	31/12/1916
War Diary	Pommier	01/01/1917	08/03/1917
War Diary	Grenas	09/03/1917	13/03/1917
War Diary	Bayencourt	14/03/1917	31/03/1917
War Diary	St. Hilaire	01/04/1917	13/04/1917
War Diary	Bethune	14/04/1917	18/04/1917
War Diary	Lievin	19/04/1917	24/04/1917
War Diary	Bully-Grenay	25/04/1917	29/04/1917
War Diary	Lievin	30/04/1917	30/04/1917
Miscellaneous	H.Q's Glory	01/06/1917	01/06/1917
War Diary	Lievin	01/05/1917	12/05/1917
War Diary	Bully-Grenay	13/05/1917	19/05/1917
War Diary	Germany Front Line M10a61.70	20/05/1917	20/05/1917
War Diary	M10a61.70	21/05/1917	26/05/1917
War Diary	M16b55.95	27/05/1917	28/05/1917
War Diary	M11C18.75	30/05/1917	31/05/1917
Miscellaneous	To H.Q. 137 Bde	03/07/1917	03/07/1917
War Diary	M11C18.75	01/06/1917	15/06/1917
War Diary	Bully Grenay Map 36 B, 1/40,000	16/06/1917	21/06/1917
War Diary	Lievin M28D.78.31	22/06/1917	30/06/1917
Miscellaneous	To HQ 137 Bde	01/08/1917	01/08/1917
War Diary	Lievin M18d 78.31	01/07/1917	03/07/1917

War Diary	Reveillon V26d 30.35	03/07/1917	25/07/1917
War Diary	Drouvin Map. Ref. 36B. N.E. K.3b 6.2	26/07/1917	31/07/1917
War Diary	Drouvin K3b 6.2	01/08/1917	03/08/1917
War Diary	G23b 3.0 36c N.W.	04/08/1917	09/08/1917
War Diary	Trenches G23b 3.3 36c N.W. 1/10,000	09/08/1917	15/08/1917
War Diary	H.Q.'s G23b3.3	15/08/1917	07/09/1917
War Diary	Mazingarbe	08/09/1917	31/10/1917
Miscellaneous	To H.Q.s 137 Bde	02/12/1917	02/12/1917
War Diary	Mazingarbe	01/11/1917	30/11/1917
Miscellaneous	To H.Qs. 137 Bde Herewith War Diary Of 137th Inf G Coy. For Month Of December. 1917	01/01/1918	01/01/1918
War Diary	Mazingarbe	01/12/1917	25/01/1918
War Diary	Vendin	26/01/1918	31/01/1918
Heading	War Diary of 137th Machine Gun Coy. February 1918 46 Bn MG Corps Vol I		
War Diary		15/02/1918	15/02/1918
War Diary	Beaumetz-Lez-Aire.	16/02/1918	28/02/1918
War Diary	Vendin-Lez-Bethune	01/02/1918	09/02/1918
War Diary	Hurionville	10/02/1918	10/02/1918
War Diary	Equirre	11/02/1918	14/02/1918

WO 95/2687/2

Brigade Machine Gun Company

46TH DIVISION
137TH INFY BDE

137TH MACHINE GUN COY.

FEB 1916-FEB 1918.

Army Form C. 2118.

WAR DIARY
or
INTELLIGENCE SUMMARY 137 M.G...
(Erase heading not required.)

Instructions regarding War Diaries and Intelligence Summaries are contained in F. S. Regs., Part II. and the Staff Manual respectively. Title Pages will be prepared in manuscript.

Place	Date	Hour	Summary of Events and Information	Remarks and references to Appendices
LES MAZURES	25/2/16		Company assembled.	
	7/3/16		Company (Hinde Force)	
	11/3/16		moved to HARDINVAL	
	2/3/16		" " HEM	
	3/3/16		" " REBREUVE	
	5/3/16		" " MAGNICOURT	
	9/3/16		" " ECOIVRES	
	11/3/16		Took guns up into trenches E. of NEUVILLE-ST-VAAST.	
	12/3/16		Took over 2 guns from French	
	13/3/16		" " 6 more guns from French	
	14/3/16	5.30AM	French guns mock-attacked	
	20/4/16		Relieved by 75th Ode Machine Gun Coy.	
	21/4/16		Moved to BAILLEUL aux CORNEILLES.	
			" " IVERGNY	
	4/5/16		" " ST. AMAND	
	5/5/16		" " POMMIER	
	8/5/16		1 section went to LA HAIE, Bde HQ	
			1 section took over sector on our right from 37 Divn	
			2nd section up to trenches from LA HAIE, Bde HQ	
	11/5/16		Q.M. Stores & transport moved to SOUASTRE.	

R.W.Whit...
Lieut
Pro OC 137 M.G.C.

Army Form C. 2118.

WAR DIARY
or
INTELLIGENCE SUMMARY
(Erase heading not required.)

Place	Date	Hour	Summary of Events and Information	Remarks and references to Appendices
FONQUEVILLERS	16/5/16		Relieved by 139 Bde. & moved to GAUDIEMPRE	
	20/5/16		moved to BREVILLERS	
	4/6/16		moved to HUMBERCAMP, transport to LA BAZEQUE FARM.	
	8/6/16		Digging Cable Trenches	
	17/6/16		moved to trenches at FONQUEVILLERS	
	20/6/16		Relieved by 138 Bde. & moved to BREVILLERS.	
	22/6/16		marched to FONQUEVILLERS trenches, relieving 138 Bde.	
	24/6/16	U day	Bombardment of GOMMECOURT	During this our Machine Guns were very active firing on tracks & roads in rear of enemy lines
	25/6/16	V		
	26/6/16	W		
	27/6/16	X		
	28/6/16	Y		
		Z	2 days postponed 2 days.	
	1/7/16	Z	Day. Attack on GOMMECOURT.	

WAR DIARY
or
INTELLIGENCE SUMMARY

Army Form C. 2118.

Place	Date	Hour	Summary of Events and Information	Remarks and references to Appendices
FONQUEVILLERS	1/7/16	7/30 AM	Attack on GOMMECOURT WOOD. Our guns were assembled in dugouts about 30 yards in rear of retrenchment & were detailed to advance with 5th, 7th, & 9th Sherwoods. They did not go forward beyond our front line as the trenches were congested with men of other units. All our officers report that information was received that the wires had not been cut beyond the German front line. Half the guns of each section were therefore mounted in the old front line with the remainder in support. The two guns originally mounted S. of GOMMECOURT ROAD fired into GOMMECOURT from zero to + 30 and then proceeded to old front line N. of GOMMECOURT ROAD. Where the same information was received, & when it was apparent that no further progress was being made, these guns returned & were mounted in their original position, the officer in charge keeping in touch with the troops half of the GOMMECOURT ROAD. The system of alternate assembly tunnels (A) for the machine guns was entirely satisfactory.	

RETRENCHMENT.

ORIGINAL FRONT LINE

Geo. A. Bull
2nd Lieut.
for O.C. 1/1 Z. g. Coy

WAR DIARY
or
INTELLIGENCE SUMMARY
(Erase heading not required.)

Army Form C. 2118.

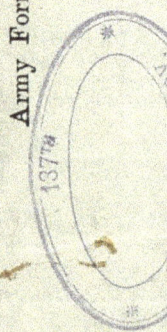

Place	Date	Hour	Summary of Events and Information	Remarks and references to Appendices
FONQUEVILLERS	July 1st		Our casualties were 2nd Lieuts. Phillips wounded, 1 man killed, 12 wounded. These were incurred in advancing to the front line, not in the attack itself.	
"	July 2		We were relieved by the 138th Machine Gun Company & proceeded to SOUASTRE	
BERLES au BOIS	July 3		We relieved the 111th Coy Machine Gun Company in trenches in front of BERLES	
"	July 6		HQ in BERLES. Pomefret at LAHERLIERE 2nd Lieut. D. Ahern & LRG Stevens joined the Company	
"	" 14		138 Coy. took over trenches 93 to 103 on our right, relieving 3 of our guns	
"	" 15		Three of our guns relieved 3 guns of 139th Coy in taking over trenches 133-140 on our left	
"	" 31		While at BERLES we have done a considerable amount of indirect fire on enemy communic. trenches, ADINFER WOOD, & the towns of RANSART and MONCHY au BOIS.	

W.A. Wray
Lieut
for OC 137 M.G. Coy

Vol 7

Confidential
War Diary.
137th Machine Gun Company
for the month of
August 1916

WAR DIARY or INTELLIGENCE SUMMARY

Army Form C. 2118.

Aug. 1916.

Place	Date	Hour	Summary of Events and Information	Remarks and references to Appendices
BERLES AU BOIS.	1/8/16	night	Ref. RANSART map 1/10,000. We fired on gups in enemy wire, and on RANSART-ADINFER ROAD.	
"	2/8/16	"	" " " Trenches & Dump X13c. with battery of 3 guns, we also fired on gups in wire.	
"	3/8/16	"	" " RANSART-ADINFER ROAD, the nose of our gun being intended to hide sounds of digging advanced trench W12c53 to W12b63.	
"	4/8/16	—	We commenced a long tunnel out into No mans Land, in front of 116 trench, where we intended making an emplacement.	
"	5/8/16	night	Fired on MONCHY and RANSART-ADINFER ROAD.	
"	"	night	In conjunction with Artillery we swept trenches & trenches behind where our new gun was to take place. We started a new emplacement at GASTINEAU. 2/Lt. H.G. Hall joined this Company.	
"	6/8/16	"	Fired on MONCHY.	
"	7/8/16	"	In conjunction with 128 M.G. Coy., we fired on trenches W29 b23 to W29 b56.	
"	8/8/16	"	We also fired on Dump X13c.	
"	9/8/16	"	We did but first fire for few of reprisals our working party.	
"	10/8/16	12:30 am	For some reason our fire was limited to sweeping party. Lt. S.J. Houston wounded 1 OR killed by shell while keeping gun in enemy wire 2:15-5 AM.	
"	11/8/16	—	Six reinforcements from M.G. Corps. Fired on RABBIT WOOD ROAD, DUMP X13c to cover working party withdrawing wire & parapet at dawn.	
"	12/8/16	"	No firing on either side.	
"	13/8/16	"	Fired on ADINFER WOOD, RABBIT WOOD ROAD & concentrated 4 guns at intervals during the night on RANSART.	
"	14/8/16	—	2/Lt Sloane-Jones & 6 N.C.Os go to machine gun school Camiers.	
"	"	night	We concentrate 3 guns on Dump X13c & RANSART.	

Signed
for O.C. 157 M.G. Coy

Army Form C. 2118.

Instructions regarding War Diaries and Intelligence Summaries are contained in F. S. Regs., Part II. and the Staff Manual respectively. Title Pages will be prepared in manuscript.

WAR DIARY
or
INTELLIGENCE SUMMARY
(Erase heading not required.)

Place	Date	Hour	Summary of Events and Information	Remarks and references to Appendices
BERLES	15/8/16.	Night	Ref RANSART MAP 1/10,000. 16 men from the Battalion in 137 Bde attached to help us with Transport arrived. We fired on RANSART, 3 guns concerted to intervals, we also fired on MONCHY and swept the return dump at X13c and Road RANSART – MONCHY. It was a misty morning & we traversed enemy wire parapet till it was clear.	 for O.C. 137 M.G.Coy
"	16/8/16.	"	We fired on Ration Dump X13c, Road RANSART-MONCHY, swept enemy wire parapets at dawn.	
"	17/8/16	"	In conjunction with the artillery we fired at given times on RANSART and ROADS near RABBIT WOOD.	
"	18/8/16	"	We fired on RANSART & made tapping into there.	
"	19/8/16	"	" " enemy salient W23b & W24a in conjunction with artillery and trench mortars. We finished all blankets (anti gas) frames for dugout doors.	
"	20/8/16	"	Fired on RABBIT WOOD; dump X13c, RANSART, Road RANSART – POINT 121	
"	21/8/16	"	4 guns " " RANSART and dump X13c also RABBIT WOOD	
"	22/8/16	"	We fired on RANSART as instructed by O.C. Digging party, rose to hide sound of working party.	
"	23/8/16	Afternoon Night	Artillery fired on BLOCKHOUSE & we fired with each round. Fired on RABBIT WOOD, ADINFER WOOD Roads X14&36, Cross roads X8c 62 RANSART – ADINFER ROAD, Dump X13c 8550	

Army Form C. 2118.

WAR DIARY
or
INTELLIGENCE SUMMARY

(Erase heading not required.)

Instructions regarding War Diaries and Intelligence Summaries are contained in F. S. Regs., Part II. and the Staff Manual respectively. Title Pages will be prepared in manuscript.

Place	Date	Hour	Summary of Events and Information	Remarks and references to Appendices
BERLES	25/8/16	night	Ref. RANSART Map 1/10,000 We fired on Dump X13c	
"	26/8/16	"	We fired three guns on RANSART — RANSART-ADINFER ROAD — RABBIT WOOD & Edge of ADINFER WOOD. Today we placed a gun in LIMERICK LANE where it can shoot at men using the RANSART-ADINFER ROAD.	
"	26/8/16	afternoon	Fired on trades W15+ in conjunction with the artillery. The gun in LIMERICK LANE accounted for a cyclist & soldier on RANSART-ADINFER ROAD.	
"	"	night	Fired indirect on RANSART and RANSART-ADINFER ROAD & RABBIT WOOD. 2/Lt. Sidwell-Jones to hospital.	
"	27/8/16	night	LIMERICK LANE gun killed German officer on RANSART-ADINFER ROAD. We fired on RANSART and RANSART-ADINFER ROAD.	
"	28/8/16	night	LIMERICK LANE gun killed 3 men on RANSART-ADINFER ROAD We fired on road RANSART to POINT 127, Edge of ADINFER WOOD & RANSART he machine killed by indirect machine gun fire on to BERLES.	
"	29/8/16	night	We fired 3 guns on to MONCHY & also on RANSART & rod RANSART - Pt 127.	
"	30/8/16	night	2/Lt. L.R.G. Hume to hospital (strained back) Fired on new work HAMEAU FARM to BLAIRVILLE, Edge of ADINFER WOOD, & Dump X13c.	
"	31/8/16	"	" " " X13a & X1c & on a machine gun emplacement at X7c0025 which had been damaged by artillery in the afternoon.	

Signature
for O.C 137 M.G. Coy.

Army Form C. 2118.

WAR DIARY
or
INTELLIGENCE SUMMARY

(Erase heading not required.)

Instructions regarding War Diaries and Intelligence Summaries are contained in F. S. Regs., Part II and the Staff Manual respectively. Title Pages will be prepared in manuscript.

Place	Date	Hour	Summary of Events and Information	Remarks and references to Appendices
BERLES au BOIS	August 1916.		Hostile aeroplanes were exceptionally quiet — so much so that an anti aircraft gun we fixed up this was not fired. Enemy machine guns have gradually increased their indirect machine gun fire at night. Attached is a diagram of a machine gun emplacement we are commencing to make in our sector. The idea is that the emplacement should be a "strongpoint in itself". It should be capable of defence by the gun team even when an enemy has carried our trenches; the machine gun being thus enabled to fire on succeeding waves of the assaulting troops whilst, as things are at present, the first German to get into our trenches silences the guns.	C Audun Lieut for O.C. 137th Coy

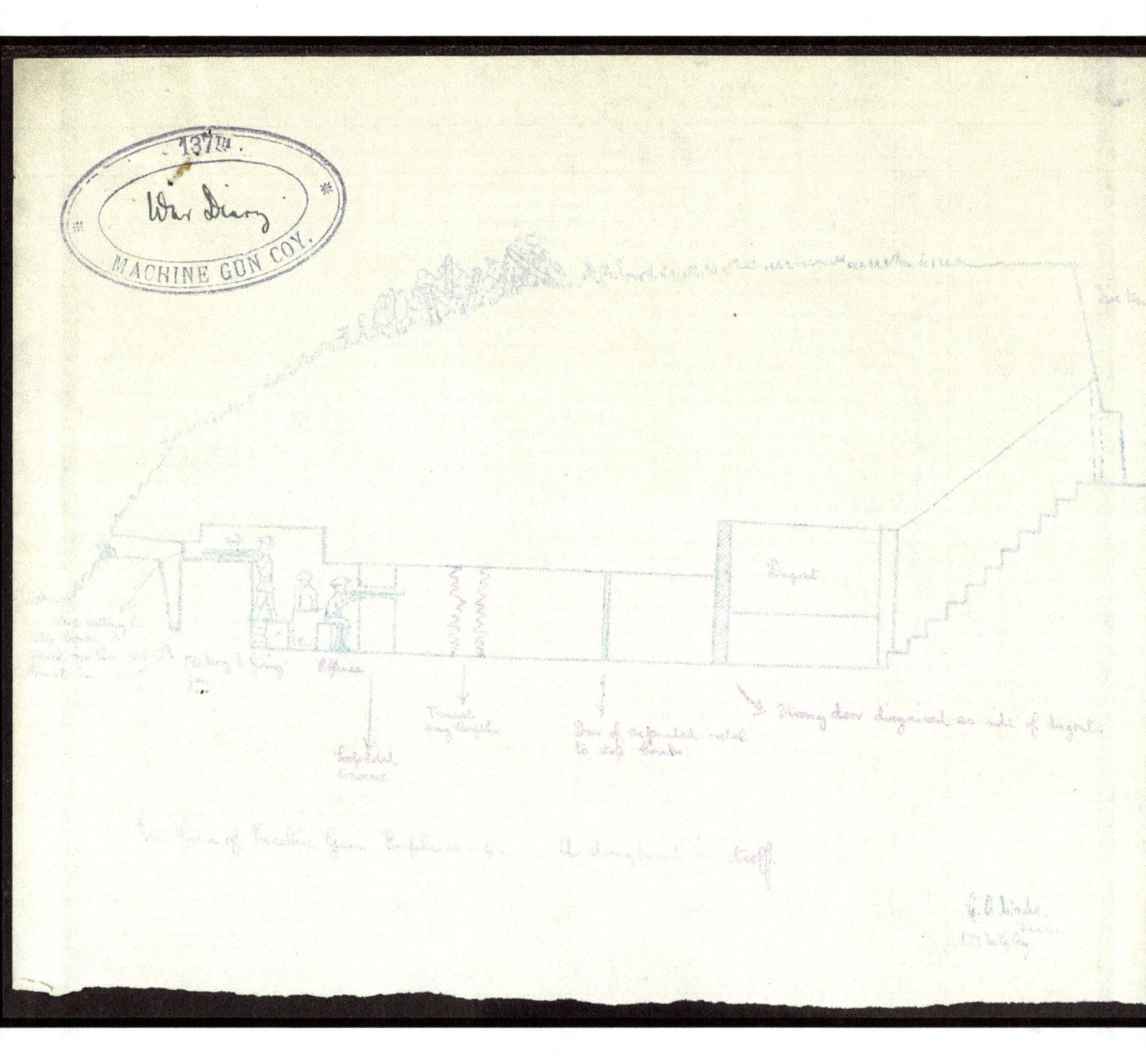

Defensive emplacement in [?].

Vol 4

Confidential

War Diary

of

137th Trench Mortar Battery.

From 1st August 1916 to 31st August 1916.

A/

137 Trench Mortar Battery
20/~~7~~ 8 17

To Brigade Major.

Report on Operations of
above battery on night of
19/20 8 16

According to instructions received
rapid fire was opened from 3
emplacements on Enemy trenches about
W 23 b 4 & b. "a a. at the following
times for 30 seconds:-
  10·11 pm.
  11·17 pm.
  1·55 am.
  2·56 am.

The enemy retaliated after the 1st
burst with one shell (probably 5·9)

After the 2nd burst of fire enemy
retaliated with 3 large Trench
Mortars which fell well over
emplacements.

After 3rd burst the enemy again
retaliated with 3 large T.M.s

After the 6th burst the enemy replied with 9 large T.M's. making 15 in all. They all fell over the support line between T 114.

The ammunition was expended as follows:-

10.11 pm.   37 rounds
11.17 pm.   39 rounds
1.55 am.   46 rounds
3.56   36 rounds
Total   158

The Rapidity of fire was well sustained. 3 mis fires occurred during operations.

R Elwood
Capt.

Army Form C. 2118.

WAR DIARY
or
INTELLIGENCE SUMMARY
(Erase heading not required.)

Instructions regarding War Diaries and Intelligence Summaries are contained in F. S. Regs., Part II. and the Staff Manual respectively. Title Pages will be prepared in manuscript.

Place	Date	Hour	Summary of Events and Information	Remarks and references to Appendices
In field.	1916. 2/8/16		All very quiet.	MAP. REF. 51 C SE. 1/10,000
"	3/8/16	7-8 pm	do. Bn. connected with proposed road. We fired 50 rounds on enemy trenches between W.24.a.23 & W.24.a.88.	
	4/8/16	5-6 pm	Bombarded by enemy trench mortars front line & C.T.s.	
	5/8/16	3 am	Bombarded on our right by hostile T.M.s (heavy & light).	
		5.30-6 pm	We fired 55 rounds on enemy front line, C.T.s.	
	6/8/16	5.30 pm	We fired 60 rounds on selected points ie Enemy trenches Gun Emplacements C.T.s. Front line Reserve line. Two salvos of 77mm. were fired at O.P.	
		11.25	In accordance with programme, 6 Stokes bombs and enemy front line C.T.s fired his front line & points selected. At 11.45 we ceased fire. 3000 rounds were fired. There was very little retaliation.	
	7.8.16		Fired all day.	
	8.8.16	Eve.	Hostile aeroplane flew very low over trenches in front of T.M. positions	
		7.30 am	Enemy shelled C.T. wrecking 2no T.M. positions. Also wounding a number of Stokes bomb footballs from our old positions. Bolos heads & Cadnage containers were blown away from the bombs but in no case did a bomb explode.	
		8 usa		
		9.20 pm	3 small T.M's unstopped to the rear of our lines in ravine at W.7.d.8.1.	
	9.8.16	5-6 pm	Enemy fired 18 small T.M's from W.23.b.5.9 & W.23.b.2.8. Also a few 77 mm. Our mortars retaliated with about 30 shell.	
	10.8.16		All very quiet.	

WAR DIARY
or
INTELLIGENCE SUMMARY
(Erase heading not required.)

Instructions regarding War Diaries and Intelligence Summaries are contained in F.S. Regs., Part II. and the Staff Manual respectively. Title Pages will be prepared in manuscript.

Army Form ____

Place	Date	Hour	Summary of Events and Information	Remarks and references to Appendices
	11-8-16	5 a.m.	Enemy shelling was heavy in front of our front line portals, followed by Machine Gun fire. One shot from Stokes caused fire to cease	
		6.30 a.m.	Enemy fired German T.M. bombs, dropped in Ravine about W. 23.1.5.9. We retaliated. Two to each on fire.	
		2.30	Enemy again dropped 12 T.M's on our trenches & Ravine. We retaliated with 30 rounds of Stokes.	
		7 p.m.	Enemy were active with Rifle Grenades & T.M's to which we retaliated.	
	12-8-16	11.30 p.m.	Enemy T.M's bombarded Ravine at W. 23.1.6.9. afterwards creeping back to on front line. Otmer & Hyper 10 fired on front line. We retaliated with 38 bombs.	
	13-8-16	2.15 p.m.	Enemy T.M's opened fire on our front line trenches. We retaliated with two Stokes bombs firing 30 rounds.	
		4-6 p.m.	Enemy T.M's dropped to the West of our hostile T.M. we retaliated. W. 24.a.3.u. when hostile T.M. was suspected. After 10 shots of T.M. Pt. hostile fire ceased. Smoke was observed to rise from some butts afterwards.	
	14-8-16	3.30 p.m.	Very quiet all day. Enemy fired one T.M. to which we retaliated.	
		11.30 p.m.	Several rounds were fired at Enemy Patrol. Observer reported that three appeared to be affected.	
	15-8-16	12 noon	Enemy bombarded our front line with T.M's. We retaliated. Two bombs for every one fired. Trench Mortar. 10 rounds at 2 hour intervals until 3.15 p.m. & we re fired 80 rounds.	
	16-8-16	3-7 p.m.	Boche T.M. were active all afternoon. We fired 82 rounds & retaliated on suspected targets.	

2449 Wt. W14957/Mg0 750,000 1/16 J.B.C. & A. Forms/C.2118/12.

Army Form C. 2118.

WAR DIARY
or
INTELLIGENCE SUMMARY
(Erase heading not required.)

Instructions regarding War Diaries and Intelligence Summaries are contained in F.S. Regs., Part II. and the Staff Manual respectively. Title Pages will be prepared in manuscript.

Place	Date	Hour	Summary of Events and Information	Remarks and references to Appendices
	17th.	5.15.	Enemy fired 5 T.M. on at hour but trenches. he fired 12 rounds in retaliation.	
	18th.	4 — 7pm	Enemy opened fire with heavy T.M. & 9 rifle grenades on our trenches. Enemy shell line he hit a grenade store with out doing any damage. he retaliated with 31 bombs.	See A.
	19.	-	Our Artillery bombarded Enemy trenches. During the night we fired Report hints to prevent enemy working on trench.	
	20th.	"	Quiet all day.	
	21.	"	do.	
	22nd.	"	do.	
	23rd.	7.30.	do. he bombarded enemy hot line in connection with Infantry Raid by 139th Brigade on our left. There were no repts to Hostile Guns. he fired 52 rounds in all	
	24th	-	Quiet all day - took on colonies or Emplacement.	
	25th.	-	Quiet all day.	
	26.	"	do.	
	27th.	"	do.	work on emplacements.
	28th	"	do	
	29th.	"	do	
	30th.	"	do	
	31st.	"	do	

X A Wood Capt
O/C 137 — 1. M. Battery

VOL 8

CONFIDENTIAL

War Diary
of
137th Machine Gun Company.

from 1st September 1916. to 30th September 1916.

WAR DIARY or INTELLIGENCE SUMMARY

Army Form C. 2118.

137 MGC

Ref RANSART MAP 1/10,000

Place	Date	Hour	Summary of Events and Information	Remarks and references to Appendices
BERLES	1/9/16	Night	Our Machine Guns fired on light Rly X13a, track from RANSART, X7d 10. RANSART-ADINFER RD = main trench at X13a.	
	2-9-16	"	In support of Raid by 1/6 South Staffd Regt on Enemy trenches W25d.81/4. to W23c.86.00. we had 11 guns firing assisted by 2 guns of 138 M.G. Coy. We fired 23,000 rounds. 4 138 M.G.Coy 6,500. The raid was successful. 1 Officer, 2 M.C.O's & 2 men being captured. Enemy machine gun very quiet, there was no retaliation on our guns.	
	3-9-16	Day	Reinforced 2nd Lt Jeffers Oct 1445 km Enemy working party seen through the mist at Quarry was dispersed by No 1 gun. Range 1,700 yards.	
		Night	Our machine guns did the usual indirect firing on enemy dumps & tracks as well as firing on gap in enemy wire made by raiding party.	
	4-9-16	Day	Started sniping with 1 Vickers Gun on RANSART-ADINFER RD range 1700 yds. 7·10 P.M. wounded a cyclist on this road. He was observed to crawl into trench. Obtained road made & wounded one man.	
		Night	Combined Artillery, T.M & M.G. strafe on enemy salient in W23 t. from 9.30 to 10 pm with surprise bursts from 10·25 – 10·30 pm. We had 12 guns firing on salient & tracks in C.T.'s behind. Retaliation on our guns slight.	
	5-9-16	Day	Sniping on R-A Rd. wounded one man.	
		Night	Fired in conjunction with artillery on Trench Rlys. X19 & X13. 10·5 pm Enemy retaliated on Ravine gun with shells & machine gun fire.	
	6-9-16	Day	Visibility too low to do anything with the LIMERICK LANE gun on RANSART-ADINFER RD & Pt. 127.	
		Night	Our guns night fire fired on Dump X13a RANSART-ADINFER RD.	

WAR DIARY
or
INTELLIGENCE SUMMARY

Army Form C. 2118.

Place	Date	Hour	Summary of Events and Information	Remarks and references to Appendices
BERLES			Ref. RANSART MAP 1/10,000.	
	7-9-16	11.30am	Heliographing observed on ridge to right of R-A.Rd. near Low Ser. Results of enemy M.G.	
		night	Indirect fire up on RANSART VILLAGE, new trench in X7c, RANSART-3 MAISONS RD in X8.	
	8-9-16	4.20pm	Man seen on R-A.Rd, when fired on fell into trench on Rt of road. Man crossing field to right of road was hit + crawled into trench. 2nd Lt Jayman reported evacuated on 3.5.9.16.	
		night	He fired on gates in enemy wire, also RANSART VILLAGE. Dump in X19a.	
	9-9-16	12.50pm	Cyclist riding up R-A.Rd was hit + fell off cycle Afterwards he crawled into jan. 4.22pm man in blue overalls, slack + round cap hit.	
		night	He fired on Dump X13c. RANSART VILLAGE. RANSART-3 MAISONS RD. RANSART-ADINFER RD.	
	10-9-16	10-10am	2 men walking up R-A.Rd. One hit, the other ran away. 5.10 PM Man coming from top of road was hit.	
		night	1 O.R. evacuated. Harrel indirect fire at night on RANSART VILLAGE + Dump X13c.	
	11-9-16	7.20pm	A man, apparently drunk, seen coming down R-A Rd. Fired at, he dived into grass on side of road but got up and staggered down the road.	
		night	He fired on Dump at X13c. can new work in X7c + X7d.	
	12.9.16	2-40pm	Man walking down R-A.Rd was hit and lay for ½ an hour. 5.30pm Man in light blue uniform hit + lay for 5 minutes then crawled into trench.	
		night	He fired as last night on Dump X13c & new work X7c. 3rd night in succession no enemy M.G. fire	

WAR DIARY
or
INTELLIGENCE SUMMARY
(Erase heading not required.)

Army Form C. 2118.

Place	Date	Hour	Summary of Events and Information	Remarks and references to Appendices
BERLES			REF RANSART MAP 1/10,000.	
	13-9-16	3.20pm	Enemy officer sniped on R-A Rd lay for a long time. 4 P.M. man in Blue grey uniform & forage cap hit & apparently killed. 6.35 pm two men walking up road fired on & hit. One was afterwards dragged off the road by the other. Lt Wade transferred to Grantham.	
		night	M.G. fired on RABBIT WOOD, C.T. in X13 a & X18a. S.A.A. work at X7a.	
	14-9-16	12.20pm	Men walking up R-A Rd was hit and tried to crawl into chalk pit, but could not, as crawled into trench on other side of Rd. Reinforcement 2nd Lt Stock + H.D.S. Lt Snowball transferred to 1/M Bay.	
		night	M.G. fired on track x7d.7.8 RANSART.VILL. + C.T. x 8c.6.2.10.	
	15-9-16	Day	Very little movement on R-A Rd. Wheel tracks were seen on surface of the road. Reinforcement 1.O.R + Lt. DAWSON vice Lt Wade.	
		night	M.G. fired on R-A Rd. RABBIT.WOOD. DUMP X13 c + ADINFER WOOD.	
	16.9.16	7.30pm	Man walking up R-A Rd out of RANSART. was hit and lay on road till dusk. 1. O.R. evacuated.	
		night	M.G. fired on again enemy mine. M.S. loophole at x7 E.15.9.5 + C.T. in X14 e. Motor transport heard in RANSART during the night.	

WAR DIARY
or
INTELLIGENCE SUMMARY
(Erase heading not required.)

Army Form C. 2118.

Place	Date	Hour	Summary of Events and Information	Remarks and references to Appendices
BERLES			Ref RANSART MAP 1/10,000	
	17.9.16	9.30am	Man hit on R-A Rd crawled across road into trench.	
		night	We fired on HAMEAU FARM. RANSART VILL. MONCHY VILL. R-A Rd CT.M × 14e & Track W30a	L/Cpl
	18.9.16	Day	Sniping by gun on R-A Rd during the day had no results. Night firing position at Sn/Cpl	
			GASTINEAU shelled with 62 shells sizes 4.5 + 5.9. They were painted yellow but no traces of gas were found.	
			Reinforcement 1 OR	
		night	We fired on CT.M × 19c & R-A Rd	L/Cpl
	19.9.16	Day	Visibility too bad for sniping. Cpl Edwards is transferred to Grantham.	
		Night	In conjunction with raid by 1/5 North Staffs Reg. we fired on Support trench × C. Front	L/Cpl
			line W18.d. Dump × 13c. Rd Junc × 19a	
	20.9.16	Day	Only two men seen on R-A Rd all day.	L/Cpl
		Night	We fired on New CT.M × 25 a & d. R-A Rd. Point 127 & RANSART VILL.	L/Cpl
	21.9.16	6.10 pm	Two men walking up R-A Rd. We hit one. The other jumped into trench & afterwards pulled	L/Cpl
			fired man in to his post.	
		Night	We fired on HAMEAU FARM. Rd × 8f. TR.Junc × 3e 33. & × 3c 5.5. MONCHY & enemy wire	L/Cpl
	22.9.16	2.50am	Man walking up road was hit & crawled into trench. 2.18 pm Another man hit, could	
			not get into trench so crawled down the road.	L/Cpl

WAR DIARY or INTELLIGENCE SUMMARY

Army Form C. 2118.

Place	Date	Hour	Summary of Events and Information	Remarks and references to Appendices
BEETLES			Ref. RANSART MAP 1/10000	
			2 O.R. evacuated.	
	23.9.16	night	M.G. fired on Light Rly. X19a. Rd. X8c7,5.35 + X8c.10.55. + RANSART. VILL	
		Day	Only one man seen on R-A Rd. We missed him.	
		night	M.G. fired on gap in wire WILT. C.T. in X25a.Y. C.T. in X14c @ Dump in X13c. Rd. X29d. Tracks in W30a.	
	24.9.16	3.30pm	A man was seen at hole in O.P. at W29b.45.55. On being fired at he disappeared	
		night	M.G. fired on gap in wire W18b. RANSART. VILL. R-A RD X14b40.8. Dump X13c7.3. - Rd. june. X19a 9.5.65.	
	25.9.16	Day	Several men were seen on the R-A Rd during the day. At 5.30 P.M. we fired at 3 men. Two hurried into trench, the other was not seen again. At 6 P.M. we fired on two men, one was killed, the other escaped.	
		Night	M.G. fired on Light Rly. X19a - X26a. RANSART. VILL. & gap in enemy wire W18b63.50	
	26.9.16	Day	No men were seen on R-A Rd during the day.	
		Night	M.G. fired on Rd. X8d2.065. Support line X7.d.44. RANSART.VILL. Rd. X8c65.30. Rd. X8c.62. Rd. X8c.45.00. + enemy front line X7d1.3. to the S.W.	

Army Form C. 2118.

WAR DIARY
or
INTELLIGENCE SUMMARY
(Erase heading not required.)

Instructions regarding War Diaries and Intelligence Summaries are contained in F.S. Regs., Part II and the Staff Manual respectively. Title Pages will be prepared in manuscript.

Place	Date	Hour	Summary of Events and Information	Remarks and references to Appendices
BERLES			Ref. RANSART MAP. 1/10,000.	
	27.9.16	Day	Only two men were observed on R-A Rd. We fired on those. He fired on Light Railway x19a to x26a. Enemy wire W18d. 63.50. CT. x13d 45.25. & Rd x14b 60.85.	
		Night	Sgt Starbuck to N.K. for Commissn.	
	28.9.16		Only one man was seen on the R-A Rd throughout the day.	
		Night	He fired on track x13c94. RANSART-MONCHY Rd x13d. Road x8c62 & got in enemy wire W18d.63.50.	
	29.9.16	Day	Only one man seen on R-A Rd. He fired on him & he disappeared on the right of the road.	
		Night	He fired on Enemy wire g.r./p. W18d.63.50. Newroofs x7c73. Track x19a g 500. Rd in RANSART X8C 4500. RANSART–ADINFER Rd. x14 b 3065.	
	30.9.16	Day	No movement was observed on the R-A Rd throughout the day.	
		Night	At 9 pm the enemy opened rapid rifle fire & thumbouts, trying to disperse our wiring parties in front of 105 & 106 trench. At 10.55 pm our guns in right sector received the message "Berles got loose"; a box respirators were worn till the O.K. message was received. Skirmishers were heard on R-A Rd at 11.35 pm when two guns promptly opened fire. Headquarters CR. Rds. x7a9g. ORRds x3c62. R-A Rd. X14b.3065. R-A Rd. x14b 60.85 & g.o.f. in wire W18d.63.50.	

War Diary
of
137th Machine Gun Coy

Confidential

Date. 1st Oct. 1916. to
31st Oct. 1916.

WAR DIARY or INTELLIGENCE SUMMARY

Army Form C. 2118.

of 137th Machine Gun Coy. from 1st Oct 1916 To 31st Oct 1916

Vol 9

Place	Date	Hour	Summary of Events and Information	Remarks and references to Appendices
BERLES			REF. MAP. RANSART. 1/10,000	
	1-10-16	Day	3	
		5.10pm	Observed from trench 140. Cyclist observed descending the hill on R-A Rd. We fired & the cyclist fell off his machine into ditch at side of road. Owing to the light failing it is not known whether he afterwards transferred was heard on R-A Rd & the gun in trench 140 that at KANARS, both opened fire 8.10pm. Again transfered was heard on the R-A Rd during the road. Guns again opened fire. Total rounds expended from both guns 3,000. We also fired on Sapin enemy wire W18 f 63.50. Dump X13 c.7.3. Rd junction X19 d.95.65. R-A Rd. X14 t.30.65.- X14 t.30.85. + Railway. X19 a - X26 a Dump X13 c.7.3. Rd junction X19 d.95.65. R-A Rd. X14 t.30.65.- X14 t.30.85. + Railway. X19 a - X26 a 5/30	
	2-10-16	Day	Visibility too bar for any observation on the R-A Rd during the day. Reinforcement 1 O.R.	
		Night	No fires indirect on to track X19 a.7.3. - X19 d.2.3. Track X13 d.13. Rd + track X7 a 48.20. and Enemy Listening Post.	3/30
	3-10-16	Day	5.20 pm 3 women observed going up the RANSART-ADINFER Rd, they were carrying something. Our machine gun opened fire & men fell on route & were not seen to move again. 1 O.R. Transferred to Base, Staples, in charge	
		Night	11 pm Enemy Field Battery spotted at X19 d.4.6. This was observed from our M.G. Position (W13 d.99.5) this battery appears to fire on our left front. We fired direct on gap in enemy wire W13 f 13.50, + indirect on Road X14 a B.R. RANSART-MONCHY Rd. X13 d.1 X13 d. also Cross Roads ad X 8 c 6.2.	3/49

2449 Wt. W14957/M90 750,000 1/16 J.B.C. & A. Forms/C.2118/12.

WAR DIARY or INTELLIGENCE SUMMARY

Army Form C. 2118.

137 M Gun Co

Place	Date	Hour	Summary of Events and Information	Remarks and references to Appendices
REF. MAP. RANSART 1/10000	4.10.16	Day	11.40am. A man observed walking up RANSART-ADINFER Rd to RANSART. Our machine gun opened fire & he fell on the left of road. We fired again & he crawled down road on his hands & knees. He was evidently hit. 1.40 pm. Observed 7 or 8 men walking across the top of road. Gun did not fire at so it would have been ineffective at the range. 5.30 pm. Observed two men walking up the road, one behind the other. We fired - first man fell face downwards. We fired at the other who fell & crawled into side of road. The first man remained where he fell & did not move again.	4.10.16
	5.10.16	Night	He fired direct on S.P.m vw W.18.t.63.55 & induced on New Enemy work x7.e1 x7.d. Trench + Rly x10.d.30.55. Dump x13.c.34 Road + Trench x8.c.11.50.0. + RANSART-ADINFER Rd Standford x14.b.00.55	
		Day	7.4 am. He observed one man walking up the RANSART-ADINFER Rd. He fired & he staggered into the left side of the road, undoubtedly hit.	
		Night	Transport were heard on the R-A Rd at 9.40 pm. One gun in our front line opened direct fire at 1,800 yds. On hearing this signal, a gun at LANARK induced position, opened fire & reached the road. We also fired direct on gap in enemy wire Nw.t.63.57. + in conjunction with a card M.7th. 138th Brigade, we fired on Enemy parapet at W.23.t.1.d, W.23.d, W.29.d.0.5. + E.5.b.45.60.	5.10.16
	6.10.16	Day	From 4.30 pm to 5.30 pm the enemy sent about seven heavy trench mortar bombs into the Ravine. Nothing was observed on the RANSART-ADINFER Rd during the day.	

Army Form C. 2118.

WAR DIARY
or
INTELLIGENCE SUMMARY
(Erase heading not required.)

137 M. Gun Co

Place	Date	Hour	Summary of Events and Information	Remarks and references to Appendices
REF. MAP. RANSART. 1/10,000	6.10.16	Night	We fired on Gaps in Enemy wire west. Lightly x19d - x26a. Rd + Rly x19d 35.55. Dump x13c 85.85. Trench x13d 40.25 + Road Rly Track x19a 9.65.	G.W.D.
	7.10.16	Day	Only two men appeared on the RANSART - ADINFER Rd during the day. We fired on these. The enemy shelled the junction of LINCOLN LANE + Trench line ad 6. a.m. 1 O.R (C.S.M.) Evacuated to Ed Pt.	
		Night	Six of our machine guns fired into RANSART VILLAGE at night, keeping up a continuous fire from 6.30 pm to 3.30 am. We also fired into gap in Enemy wire W18d 63.50.	G.W.D.
	8.10.16	Day	10. a.m. Two men seen on the RANSART. ADINFER Rd. We opened fire on then + one dropped, apparently killed. The other bolted back towards RANSART.	
		Night	We fired on Road x14a 3.5. Track x13c6.18. Track + Rd. x13d 25.15. Cross Roads x18c 6.2. + Gaps in enemy wire W18d. x7a 30. + x7a 1.9.	G.W.D.
	9.10.16	Day	A few light Trench Mortar Bombs were fired into the Ravine at ard 2.30 pm. At 4.30 p.m. we hid one man on the RANSART- ADINFER Rd. Our men dragged into a Trench by two men who were with him. The Enemy heavily shelled BERLES with 5.9 + 4.2 Shells during morning + night.	
		Night	We fired on gaps in enemy wire W18d, Track x13d 85.52. Track x13d 15.25 + the RANSART - ADINFER Rd.	G.W.D.
	10.10.16	Day	4. O.R Reinforcements. The enemy again shelled BERLES until our aircraft appeared in the morning's again during the night. Machine Guns were used directed on	G.W.D.

Army Form C. 2118.

WAR DIARY
or
INTELLIGENCE SUMMARY
(Erase heading not required.)

137 M June Co

Place	Date	Hour	Summary of Events and Information	Remarks and references to Appendices
REF MAP. RANSART. 1/10,000	11.10.16	Night	A cyclist appeared on the RANSART-ADINFER Rd at 4.50 pm. We opened fire on him & he fell into the middle of the road, undoubtedly killed. We fired on Saps in Enemy wire W.18.k. N.25 worth X.7.c.82. Junction of track & trench X.13.d.5.5.13. Road junction X.8.c.6.5.33. BLAIRVILLE-RANSART Rd X.8.d.10.32. – on the RANSART-ADINFER Rd X.14.k.30.65.	
		Day	There was considerable movement on the RANSART-ADINFER Rd during the day. Our machine gun wounded one man at 9 am. He was seen to struggle into a trench, assisted by another man. Situation in the village of BERLES was quiet throughout day & night.	
		Night	We did the usual indirect fire, our targets for the night being RANSART VILLAGE (3 guns) Dump & tracks X.13.c.86. Tracks & Lights Railway X.19.a.80.98.	
	12.11.16	Day	At 9.50 am One man was seen on the RANSART-ADINFER Rd in F.8.M.O. We fired on him and he fell into the grass on the side of the road. At 3.15pm. Two men were seen rolling up the road. We opened fire and both men dropped. Eventually one man carried the other on his back into RANSART.	
		Night	In conjunction with Trench Mortar Bombardment, we fired as the following times 10-10.10 pm 10.15 – 10.24 pm 12 midnight – 12.30 am & 1 am – 1.30 am on the following targets enemy front line as	

Army Form C. 2118.

WAR DIARY
or
INTELLIGENCE SUMMARY
(Erase heading not required.)

137th M[achine] Gun Co[mpany]

Place	Date	Hour	Summary of Events and Information	Remarks and references to Appendices
REF. MAP. RANSART 1/10,000			N.23.d.85.00, X.7.b.46.65. W.18.d & W.18.d.50.87. C.T.R. X.13.a.12.58. Road X.7.b.20.15. C.T.R. 42.H & 32.72. Cross Rds X.8.C.05.70. C.T.R. W.24.a.65.02. & Support Trench V.7.a 35.55. Green lights were sent up from the Bn enemy lines when our M.Guns opened fire. About 35. 77m/m shells were sent about 108 yards, very close to our M.G. position. No damage to our position was done.	
13.10.17	Day		Only one man, a cyclist, was observed on the RANSART Rd during the day. We fired on him & he fell off his machine.	
	Night		We fired on gaps in enemy wire wick Mesnorth X.7.C.c.4. tX.7.d.2.3. Track X.19.a.9.0. to X.19.d.35.45. Dump X.13.c.86. & on the RANSART – ADINFER Rd when transport were heard.	G/W.B.
14.10.17	Day		The enemy heavily shelled BERLES during the morning, using 5.9 & H.2 and shells as 4.15 am – till 9.45 am. commenced sending enemy shells at six three minute intervals. About 9.15 am – till 9.45 am. he sent an intense fire into the centre of the Village. During this period, a H.2 shell entered our Orderly Room. This an (8nd) shell slid decided and explode and very little damage was done, no casualties occurred at 9.45 am he slackened his fire & continued sending single shells into the village until 1.30 p.m.	G/W.B.

Army Form C. 2118.

WAR DIARY
or
INTELLIGENCE SUMMARY
(Erase heading not required.)

137th M.G.Co.

Place	Date	Hour	Summary of Events and Information	Remarks and references to Appendices
REF. MAP. RANSART. 1/10,000.	15.10.16		No further shelling of the village during the day or night. No casualties occurred in the company. During the day several men were seen on the RANSART Rd. We fired on three other observed, & caused the following casualties. One man killed & three wounded. One of the wounded men was a cyclist/cycledist, who? During the night, we fired on Sap in enemy wire W18A. Machine gun emplacement, Tracks X 13d 25.15. Road X 8C 62. also on X14A 3.8 & X13C 6.018. One cyclist was observed riding along the RANSART ADINFER Rd at 11.15 am. We fired on him & he fell off his machine, being wounded in the arm.	
		Night	(At night) we fired on Sap in enemy wire, W18A. RANSART X7d 55.72. RANSART-MONCHY Rd. X13d. & RANSART-ADINFER Rd. X14d 085 - X14d 30.65.	
	16.10.16	Day.	A grey coloured motor car was observed on the RANSART Rd at 8.10 pm. We fired on it and it swerved into side of road, but continued its journey into RANSART. It flew a white flag & had a glass screen.	
		Night.	We fired on RANSART-ADINFER Rd. Track W30 a 1.5. W24c 35.52. X19c 5.20. X29.9.92. X M30e12.92. We hoped to catch the Germans, who were returning, by firing on these Tracks, CTs & Roads.	

WAR DIARY or INTELLIGENCE SUMMARY

Army Form C. 2118.

137th M Jund C.

Place	Date	Hour	Summary of Events and Information	Remarks and references to Appendices
REF MAP RANSART 1/10,000	17.10.16	Day	A car was seen coming down the RANSART-ADINFER Rd into RANSART at 12.30 pm. It was flying the Red Cross flag. We did not fire. At 1.10 pm it was seen returning.	
		Night	We fired indirect on X7d89. X8c62. & X8d13	J.W.D
	18.10.16	Day	At 11.2 am, 3 men were seen coming up the RANSART-ADINFER Rd. We fired on them and they jumped into a shallow trench on left side of road. 12.46 pm. A Red. Cross car observed coming into RANSART. At 1.30 pm it was seen to be returning to ADINFER. 1 O.R. evacuated	J.W.D
		Night	In conjunction with a raid by 138" Bde on Enemy front line E5a13.7) – E5a11.38 and E5c07.5 – E5c62.82, we fired on two Enemy Trenches W23d4. W29d.0.5 d E5d57.50. We fired from Zero (6.30 pm) until Artillery fire ceased. No observations. Visibility too low.	J.W.D
	19.10.16	Day	We fired indirect into RANSART X8c65.33. & on to the BLAIRVILLE – RANSART Rd X8b09.19. At 10 pm the enemy sent up Golden Starlights in the direction of RANSART.	J.W.D
	20.10.16	Day	Several men were seen during the afternoon on the RANSART-ADINFER Rd. Our guns fired on them but no hits were observed.	
		Night	We fired on RANSART-MONCHY Rd X14a25.7 – X19a98.70. & on RANSART-ADINFER Rd X8c12 – X14b30.65	J.W.D J.W.D

Army Form C. 2118.

WAR DIARY or INTELLIGENCE SUMMARY
(Erase heading not required.)

137th Infn. Bde.

Place	Date	Hour	Summary of Events and Information	Remarks and references to Appendices
REF. MAP. RANSART 1/10,000.	21.10.16	Day	Only three men were observed on the RANSART-ADINFER Rd during the day. One was wearing a white band on his arm & carried a light coloured haversack.	
		Night	We fired on RANSART-MONCHY Rd X14A25.70 – X13d43 and on the RANSART-ADINFER Rd X8C62 – X14 b.3065. Four red lights were observed in the direction of BLAIRVILLE at between 7 & 8 pm.	J.W.D
	22.10.16	Day	Two men were observed on the RANSART-ADINFER Rd during the day. They were concealed when fired on. They jumped into trench on side of road. We moved our gun and team from M.G Position (Ravine) into Sap: emplacement. 2 O.R. reinforcements. Very misty all day.	J.W.D
		Night	We fired on RANSART-MONCHY Rd, RANSART-ADINFER Rd, & road X8d 15.30.	
	23.10.16	Day	At 1 pm, four men were observed on the RANSART-ADINFER Rd. When fired on, they jumped into trench on side of road. 2 O.R. reinforcements. 10.5 pm, two green lights observed north of RANSART. Enemy sent few steam T.M. into Ravine about 4 pm.	J.W.D
		Night	We fired on tracks & C.T. in X30 a.75.80. Tracks X19A 80.10. – X19 d.10.80. Road X14 b.30.65. Sap in enemy line W18 b.63.50. & RANSART-ADINFER Rd X14 b.30.65.	J.W.D

Army Form C. 2118.

WAR DIARY
or
INTELLIGENCE SUMMARY

(Erase heading not required.)

137th Infantry.

Place	Date	Hour	Summary of Events and Information	Remarks and references to Appendices
REF. MAP. RANSART. 1/10,000.	24-10-16	Day	Visibility too bad for observation. Between noon & 1pm, the enemy sent a large number of Medium Size Trench Mortars into Ravine. Also two or three salvoes from light field guns. At 1.50 pm enemy sent up ten Red rockets in direction of RANSART. Between 5pm & 7pm, he sent up twenty Green lights, from BLAIRVILLE.	
		Night	We fired on gap in enemy wire W.18.d.63.50. through the night. Also on the RANSART- ADINFER Rd X.14.b.30.65.	
	25-10-16	Day	A few men were seen on the RANSART-ADINFER Rd during the day. Two of them were wearing long grey overcoats and peak caps. One of them was lit by our fire.	
		Night	In conjunction with a raid by the 137th Bde on enemy trenches about W.24.a.3.4. we fired as follows:- Enemy front line W.23.b.85.05. to the south; Trench X.7.c.80.25. Frontline W.18d.4.7. Front line W.18d.65.70. to W.18d.50.85. Front line W.18.b.60.95 to W.18.b.65.12. TR.Jun. W.24.a.80.50. Supp.TR. X.13.a.15.35. CT. W.24.b.15.40. Rd. Junc: X.7.d.88.90. CT. W.24.c.75.95. Supp.TR. W.24.a.95.38. The 138th M.G.Coy. assisted with three guns, firing on W.24.c.60.25. W.24.a.65.00. enemy front line W.23.b. All guns fired from Zero – 5 minutes until artillery fire ceased (10.55pm) Zero was at 10.20 pm. 2 O.R. evacuated.	

WAR DIARY or INTELLIGENCE SUMMARY

Army Form C. 2118.

[B] M. McFarlane (?)

Place	Date	Hour	Summary of Events and Information	Remarks and references to Appendices
REF. MAP. RANSART. 1/5,000.	26/01/16	Day	At 5.35 am a motor lorry was seen on the RANSART-ADINFER Rd. On being fired at it galloped speed into the village. At 9 a.m. it was seen returning. Our artillery dealt with it. Transport road in RANSART at 10.30 pm.	J.O.D.
		Night	We fired on track T.R. X13 d 60.10. Enemy Gun Pits W24d 45.50. Track W24a 5.2. Cross Rds. X 8 c 62. 1 O.R. evacuated.	
	27/01/16	Day	2.10 pm. 8 men wearing F.S.M.D. were observed walking down RANSART-ADINFER Rd. When fired on they jumped into trench. 4.30pm. Red + Car seen going slowly into RANSART. 4.32 pm. Car (Red +) seen returning. We did not fire.	J.O.D.
		Night	We fired on RANSART-MONCHY Rd X19d 98 65. – X14a 20 75. and on track TRh X19 a9 590.	
	28/01/16	Day	NO observation during the day.	
		Night	We fired on Track v Track X13 d 55.13. – Track W24a 5.2. – on RANSART – MONCHY Rd. X 8 c 7.14. – X14 a 20.75.	J.O.D.
	29/01/16		Company relieved from trenches by 21st M. Sgn. Relief started at 10.30 am and was completed at 4 pm. Three sections of our Company billeted in Canteen, BERLES + one section at H.Q.	
	30/01/16		Company commenced march at 10.30 am to BRAIVILLERS. Order of march was by sections at 20 minutes interval. Route taken was via LA CAUCHIE, GOMBREMETZ, HOMBERCOURT, LUCHEUX.	

Army Form C. 2118.

WAR DIARY
or
INTELLIGENCE SUMMARY

137th Infantry Co.

(Erase heading not required.)

Place	Date	Hour	Summary of Events and Information	Remarks and references to Appendices
			REF. MAP. LENS II. 1/100,000.	
			BRAIVILLERS. Dinner was taken at GOMBREMETZ. The company marched splendidly, arriving in Billets at 5 p.m. 1. O.R. Reinforcement just	
BRAIVILLERS	31.10.16		Company spent day packing limbers, cleaning billets etc. just	

Army Form C. 2118.

WAR DIARY or **INTELLIGENCE SUMMARY**
(Erase heading not required.)

137 M. Gun Co.   Vol 10

Place	Date	Hour	Summary of Events and Information	Remarks and references to Appendices
BREVILLERS	1.11.16		REF. MAP. LENS 11. 1/100,000. Company paraded at 5.45 am. Marched as a Company via La SOUICH, BOUQUEMAISON and BONNIERS to FORTEL, arriving there about 9 am. Roads very good, men marched well. 3 pm parade for cleaning guns etc.	
FORTEL	2.11.16		Cleaning up billets, repacking limbers etc.	
"	3.11.16		Company fell in 7am & marched off at 7.15 am. Arrived at HANCHY at 1 pm. Route taken was via AUXI.LE.CHATEAU & HEIRMONT.	
HANCHY	4.11.16		Company drilling on parade field in morning. Football matches in afternoon.	
	5.11.16		Church Parade at 10.30 am. Company marched off 9.30 am. Football training in afternoon.	
	6.11.16		Route March with 8 Gun limbers from 10.15–12.30 pm. 5.30–8.30. Officers mounted for night Reconnaissance. Compass Work. Very wet. I.O.R. Reinforcement. I.O.R. Evacuated	
	7.11.16		6 am – 1 pm. March & training in Rangetaking, Indicator & Recognition of angles etc. Football in afternoon. Company canteen opened. Still very wet.	
	8.11.16		I.O.R. Reinforcement. Company in training during morning, afternoon.	
	9.11.16		Company paraded in morning for Close Order Drill.	
	10.11.16		Morning Parade. Full Coy Inspection with transport. Rapid packing of limbers show rendered	

Army Form C. 2118.

WAR DIARY
or
INTELLIGENCE SUMMARY
(Erase heading not required.)

137 M. Gun Co.

Place	Date	Hour	Summary of Events and Information	Remarks and references to Appendices
	10.11.16	Cont.	Afternoon. Football match v. Bde H.Q. The Coy won. 7-4. 1 O.R. evacuated	M
	11.11.16		Coy paraded at 7 am to march to MARCHEVILLE. En route, the coy practised plan of attack on training ground. Reached MARCHEVILLE about 3pm.	M
	12.11.16		Cleaning of guns, spare parts etc, also cleaning up billets. Afternoon, football.	M
	13.11.16	7am - 1pm	Close order drill & gun drill. 2.30-3.30. Officers Rangetaking. Belt cleaning.	M
	14.11.16	9.15-12.30pm	Route march by sections. Practice in choice of gun positions.	
		5.30pm	Lecture to Section Officers to men. Afternoon, football.	M
	15.11.16	9.30-12.30pm	Extended order drill with guns. Semaphore messages.	
		5-7.30pm	Night operations. Practicing the attack.	M
	16.11.16	9.15-10.15am	Semaphore. 10.30-1pm Route march through CRESSY. fired.	
		2pm	Lecture by Officers on "Errors of the day". 1 O.R. evacuated	M
	17.11.16	9.15-12.30pm	Firing on Range. 2.15pm. Route march to DONVAST.	
		5.30pm	Lecture at ARGENVILLERS on Gas. 8.11pm. A rim broke out which Coy. assisted by A.S.C. on duty till midnight, when fire was extinguished	M
	18.11.16		Owing to fire, programme of work was not carried out. Afternoon football.	M

WAR DIARY or INTELLIGENCE SUMMARY

Army Form C. 2118.

137 M. Gun Co.

Place	Date	Hour	Summary of Events and Information	Remarks and references to Appendices
	19.11.16		Church parade. Court of Inquiry re fire of 17th.	
	20th		9.15 – 10.45 am. Cleaning guns etc. 11 – 12.30 pm Close order drill. 2 – 3 pm. Route march. 5.30 – 7.0 pm. Packing & unpacking gun tripods from pack mules.	
	21st		9.15 – 10.45 am. Gun & disciplinary drill. Brigadier visited parade held during morning. 11 – 12.30 pm Indication & Recognition of targets. Afternoon, Football final.	
	22nd		Company paraded at 10. am to march to HANCHY via DOMVAST, GAPENNES & YVRENCH. Arrived about 2.30 pm.	
	23rd		Coy paraded at 8.30 am & marched to BACHIMONT. via AUXI-LE-CHATEAU. Arrived 12.15 pm. Repacking limbers. Cleaned guns etc. H.O.R. Reinforcements.	
	24th		Coy paraded at 8.30 am & marched to BREVILLERS. VIA FORTEL, BONNIERS, BOUQUEMAISON. Arrived at 2.30 pm.	
	25th		Men paraded for cleaning up billets, clothing & equipment.	
	26th		9.15 – 12.30 pm. Parade for cleaning guns, tripods etc.	
	27th		9.15 – 10.45 am Close Order drill. 2 pm Section New Box Respirators in gas chamber. 5. O.R. evacuated.	

Army Form C. 2118.

137 M Gun Co

WAR DIARY
or
INTELLIGENCE SUMMARY
(Erase heading not required.)

Instructions regarding War Diaries and Intelligence Summaries are contained in F. S. Regs., Part II. and the Staff Manual respectively. Title Pages will be prepared in manuscript.

Place	Date	Hour	Summary of Events and Information	Remarks and references to Appendices
	25th		Brigade Ceremonial Parade at 10.30 a.m. Coy fell in at 8 a.m. Dress, fighting Order, Haversack waterbottle on back. Afternoon Pay, cleaning guns &c.	
	26th	9.30 – 10.30 a.m. Ceremonial Drill. 10.45 – 11.40. Box Respirator drill 11.45 – 12.45 p.m. Gun drill. 2 p.m. Medical Inspection.	2 OR Reinforcements	

Norman Henry Lt.
f o.c. 137th M.G. Cy.

WAR DIARY
or
INTELLIGENCE SUMMARY

Army Form C. 2118.

137 Bde M Gun Co
Vol XI

Place	Date	Hour	Summary of Events and Information	Remarks and references to Appendices
BREWILLERS	1.12.16		Company paraded at 7.45 am. Dress fighting order 10.30 am. Inspection by 3rd Army Commander & O.C. 16th Division. Brigade highly complimented on its fine appearance. Afternoon Company paraded for limber washing	B/11
	2.11.16		Platoon from Regimen examined & made up new establishment Inspection by M.G. Officer 4th Corps at 11.30 am. Football in afternoon.	B/11 B/11 B/11
	3.12.16		Running drill, Box Respirator drill in the morning. Cleaning guns etc.	B/11
	4.12.16		Coy paraded to march to ST AMAND. Arrived at 11.30 am. Route taken was via LUCHEUX, LABEUVE & GAUDIEMPRE.	B/11
Map Ref RANSART 51C S.E d	5.12.16		Coy marched to POMMIER. 2 Sections relieved 2 Sections of 148th M.G. Coy in MONCHY Section. 2 Sections & Coy H.Q. at POMMIER. At anglais fired on light Rly at E.12.a.10.20.	B/11 B/11
FONQUEVILLERS 57 D.N.E. 1.10,000	6th		Cross Rds at E.5.a.9.8. + in vicinity of Church, MONCHY. Situation quiet	B/11
	7th		At night we fired on light Rly E.12.a & Cross Rds in MONCHY.	B/11
	8th		I.O.R. Reinforcement evacuated to England sick. 2nd Lieut Dawson 9.W.	B/11 B/11
	11th		We fired on MONCHY on Rly F.4.a.55.35. & MONCHY. Line Dawson 9.W. Rd Junction at E.12 & 32.10.	B/11
	12th		6.R.C. attacked from Battalion of Brigade	B/11
			8. O.R.C. arrived as reinforcements from the Base	B/11
	13th		In conjunction with bombardment of enemy lines & of village of MONCHY, we fired 9 guns onto the village & tracks leading to village. We fired at intervals from 10 am - 3 am on the 14th met. M.G. rounds fired 25,000.	B/11

WAR DIARY or INTELLIGENCE SUMMARY

Army Form C. 2118.

137th Bde M Gun Co

Place	Date	Hour	Summary of Events and Information	Remarks and references to Appendices
Ref Map FONQUEVILLERS 57 d N.E. 1/10000				
FONQUEVILLERS 57 d N.E. 1/10000	13.12.16 cont		The enemy retaliated chiefly on our front line & support trenches & at dusk sent up S.O.S. signal & put up a very heavy barrage on our sunk & in front of his own trenches. Without disclosing we were going to shoot according to orders moved all guns in section Reserve. Guns sent into dug outs & Bn Reserves were ordered to be arms. No casualties in the Company.	Appx
	14.12.16		No fire until on Gun Ranks E.56 44.12 & E.56 15.80 from dusk until 10 p.m.	Appx
	15.12.16		Fired indirect on Quarry F.7.a.50.35 also Batt. H.Q. at E.56 45.12 from 5 p.m. until 9 p.m.	Appx
	16.12.16		Indirect fire on Church Square E.56 45.40, Road Junction E.6.a.05.30 from dusk until 8 p.m.	Appx
	17.12.16		One gun indirect on Quarry F.7.a.50.35 from 7pm to 10pm.	Appx
	18.12.16		One gun fired indirect on W.29 d 7.38 from 5/p.m. 2-9 p.m.	Appx
	19.12.16		2nd Lieut Cowley J.D. arrived as reinforcement from the Base.	Appx
	20.12.16		One gun fired indirect on E.56 12.60 & machine gun damage E.56 45.12	Appx
	21.12.16		Both fired at intervals from 5 p.m. to 9 p.m.	Appx
	22.12.16		2nd Lieut Sowler L.L. joined us reinforcement from the Base.	Appx
	23.12.16		One gun fired indirect on Road Junction E.56 40.80 from 5pm to 9pm. C.Q.M.S. Sgt Harvey E. joined in from (22.D.G.) by & took up his duties with us Coy Sergt.	Appx
	24.12.16		Xmas Day. C.O. gave a dinner to the two sections at rest (One in Bay in Reserve & the other in Divisional Reserve) in the C.Q.M.S. store at 1/pm.	Appx
	25.12.16			Appx

Army Form C. 2118.

WAR DIARY
or
INTELLIGENCE SUMMARY
(Erase heading not required.)

Instructions regarding War Diaries and Intelligence Summaries are contained in F.S. Regs., Part II. and the Staff Manual respectively. Title Pages will be prepared in manuscript.

137th Bde. Bat. M.Gun Co.

Ref Map FONQUEVILLERS 57 d NE RANSART 51 c S.E. 1/10000

Place	Date	Hour	Summary of Events and Information	Remarks and references to Appendices
	25.12.16		Xmas Day (Cont.) A conspicuous report was forwarded including English Beer which will conveniently seemed to synchronize the arrival of firing three twenty down to the C.O. after which had there his best with old beef & port.	8M
			At night we had advice of an gun train on Batt. N.Q. Wonby. E 5 b 45.10 & each gun fired Shy a half at the following times:- 5.50 p.m., 6.25 p.m., 7.15 p.m., 8.30 p.m., & 9 p.m. also fired at some target at intervals between the above stated times.	8M
			The enemy in spite of above seemed to be very active, enemy's convoys & reinforcing elements to & from to him, patrol which appeared near outer cemetery. Two sections in Gardens were relieved.	8M
			Enemy artillery rather active.	8M
	26.12.16		Two sections relieved yesterday were unharmed in C.Q. Some at 1 p.m. & seemed to appreciate it even more than the other two sections.	8M
	27.12.16		Two guns fired indirect on Batt. N.Q. E 5 b 45.10, Cross Roads E 5 b 45.7.2, Chalk Square E 5 b 45.40 from 5 h.m. to 9 p.m.	8M
			One from Batt. D.Q. E 5 b 45.12.	8M
	28.12.16		One Gross Pte Ryby W. evacuated to Hospital.	8M
	29.12.16		A combined bombardment by R.A. Corps Heavy Artillery, 30" & 6" Divisional artillery was carried out today at 12 noon on enemy's front line between his trenches but little retaliation & no was received from him. At night we had two guns trained on the approaches & this part of the line. N 29 c 2.4 & W 29 c 5.0 taken for about two hours, slight damage was done.	8M

Army Form C. 2118.

WAR DIARY
or
INTELLIGENCE SUMMARY

(Erase heading not required.)

137th Bde. M.Gun Co.

Place	Date	Hour	Summary of Events and Information	Remarks and references to Appendices
Ref. Map FONQUEVILLERS 57d N.E. RANSART 51c S.E. 1/20,000	29-12-16		went also on dump intended - 21. 29. c.	B/4
	30-12-16		Last night a considerable & heavy downpour of rain, looking for several hours, effected considerable damage to our already dirty trenches, which + water up C-side thigh is quite the normal thing & in some places it is even up to the neck in water. Our of our sumps dug out contain 9 feet of water.	B/11
	31-12-16		Still raining. Our guns fired on enemy's Roads in Monchy.	B/11

E Rayburn
Lieut.
for O.C. 137 Machine Gun Coy.

WAR DIARY
or
INTELLIGENCE SUMMARY

Army Form C. 2118.

137 M.G. Coy (Sept 1917)

Place	Date	Hour	Summary of Events and Information Ref Map FONQUEVILLERS 57 N.E. RANSART 51 N.E.	Remarks and references to Appendices
Pommier	1-1-17		Enemy fired about 30 shells of different calibre indiscriminately into BIENVILLERS directly after MIDNIGHT 31-12-16.	B.M.
	5-1-17		23013 Pte. Harvey C.H. evacuated to Hospital.	B.M.
	8-1-17		21824 Pte. Morris E. evacuated to R.F. Corps.	B.M.
			Artillery of the enemy has shown more activity this last day or two, frequently shelling BIENVILLERS & occasionally POMMIER. Weather exceptionally wet & troops very unhealthy. 23414 A/Corp Hawkins W. evacuated to Hospital in England. Our many been have been firing in defence on enemy's Roads, Dumps & Batteries about Quentin and onwards. Our efforts to have had very good effect as the enemy frequently responds to our fire with very open fire with 77 m.m. shells & machine guns.	B.M.
	10-1-17		Enemy shelled POMMIER rather severely with 5.9 in. shells. The explosion at our H.Q. was completely demolished. One shell struck down street in yards from H.Q. smashing the roof & one of the walls. Although ten of our teams were next door they were unhurt. Two men in neighbouring billet (not of this company) were wounded.	B.M.
	15-1-17		21787 Pte Rudd by F.Smith (+Hospital) 8887 Pte Baldwin F.a. 1/5" South Staffs Regt, attached to this company,	B.M.

Army Form C. 2118.

WAR DIARY
or
INTELLIGENCE SUMMARY

(Erase heading not required.)

Instructions regarding War Diaries and Intelligence Summaries are contained in F. S. Regs., Part II. and the Staff Manual respectively. Title Pages will be prepared in manuscript.

Place	Date	Hour	Summary of Events and Information	Remarks and references to Appendices
PONNIER			Ref. MAP FONQUEVILLERS 57d N.E. RANSART 51c S.E. 1/10000	
	15-1-17		"Mounted at Duty." He was attended to by M.O. & given four days light duty	BDU
	17-1-17			BDU
	18-1-17		43265 Pte Robinson J arrived on reinforcement from the Base.	
			In conjunction with Artillery bombardment we fired on pillars on Enemy's Trenches, Roads, Railways etc. Rifles were synchronised & heavy bursts of fire given at its following times, from 6.30 p.m. to 7 p.m. & from 7.40 p.m. 58 p.m.	
			Targets:—	
			Quarry & Cross Roads at F 7 a	
			Junction of Tracks at E 12 b 3.3	
			Cemetery Cross Roads at E 5 d 9.9	
			Railway Junction at E 12 a 5.3	
			Cross Roads at E 6 a 15.32	
			Each of the four guns fired in all 1500 rounds.	BDU
			At 10.30 p.m. an emplacement at E 46 40.55 was blown in by Heavy Trench Mortar shell. Gun was slightly damaged but remains unknown. This was one of the guns operating as above.	BDU
	19-1-17		70513 Pte Rigby W. rejoined from the Base.	B2U
	21-1-17		Severe Frost has set in & looks likely to continue for some time.	BDU

2449 Wt. W14957/Mgo 750,000 1/16 J.B.C. & A. Forms/C.2118/12.

Army Form C. 2118.

WAR DIARY
or
INTELLIGENCE SUMMARY

(Erase heading not required.)

Instructions regarding War Diaries and Intelligence Summaries are contained in F. S. Regs., Part II. and the Staff Manual respectively. Title Pages will be prepared in manuscript.

Place	Date	Hour	Summary of Events and Information	Remarks and references to Appendices
POMMIER	23.7.17		Ref Map FONQUEVILLERS 57d N.E. RANSART 51 c S.E. 1/10000	*(sketch)* LEFT RIGHT
			Much aerial activity on both sides. Enemy planes several times crossed our lines but were driven back by A.A guns & Machine Guns. Enemy plane with markings as per memo was seen at 10.15 a.m. in mornings. Tail of plane could not be seen distinctly but it was not a fish tail.	
			42582 Pte Sandell J.S. evacuated to A.S.C Motor Transport Rouen.	Edn
			70499 Pte Richards T.G. evacuated to C.C.S.	Edn
			19261 Pte Mackenzie J.A. evacuated to C.C.S.	Edn
			31817 Pte Robinson J. evacuated to A.O.C. England.	Edn
	24.7.17		The following men arrived as reinforcements from the BASE.	
			21853 Pte Hull A.J.	Edn
			60300 Pte Bullock A.	Edn
			25041 Pte Slavey P.	Edn
			37422 Pte Loulton E.	Edn
			In conjunction with Artillery Bombardment we opened enemy lines. enemy targets as per 18-1-17 from 10.45 p.m. to 11.15 p.m. & from 12.5 a.m. to 12.20 a.m. Total guns fired in all about 1400 rounds.	Edn

Army Form C. 2118.

WAR DIARY
or
INTELLIGENCE SUMMARY
(Erase heading not required.)

Instructions regarding War Diaries and Intelligence Summaries are contained in F.S. Regs., Part II. and the Staff Manual respectively. Title Pages will be prepared in manuscript.

Place	Date	Hour	Summary of Events and Information	Remarks and references to Appendices
Ref Map FONQUEVILLERS 57d N.E. 1/20000			RANSART 57 c S.E. 1/20000	
	26-1-17		The enemy rain it attempts a raid tonight, in front of his own had been lifted to make it up. Three of our guns were slightly altered from their usual angles of fire so as to sweep the ground round about the gap in anticipation of their event, but nil reached ground.	
	27-1-17		Same precautions were taken as last night.	
	28-1-17		Same precautions were taken as in the previous two nights. No disturbance occurred.	
	30-1-17		At 10.30 a.m. the enemy exploded an enemy shell blew in the entrance to our dugout at No 3 position at E 46 40 53. One of our men was blown down the steps but besides being shaken up a bit he was practically unhurt.	

E. Ropkins
Lieut
For O.C. 137 Machine Gun Company

WAR DIARY or INTELLIGENCE SUMMARY

Army Form C. 2118.

Vol 13 137 Bn Mach Jun Co

Place	Date	Hour	Summary of Events and Information	Remarks and references to Appendices
POMMIER	1-2-17		Ref Map FONQUEVILLERS 57d N.E. 1/10000 RANSART 51c S.E. 1/10000 The 138 Machine Gun Company relieved us. 1 gun position No's 1, 4, 5 & 6 adjusted as follows. No 1. E 4 d 70·35 No 5 E 4 c 40·15 No 4 E 10 b 50·35 No 6 E 9 a 75·20 The relief was completed by 1·30 p.m. 21854 Pte Hanran H. Hospital A.S. Gunshot wnd A.O.C. 21856 " " Hospital A.S. Gunshot wnd the following positions	B.O.M.
	2-2-17		We took over from 149 Machine Gun Company on our left the following positions adjusted at H 28 b 90·40, H 23 c 60·40, H 23 b 10·00, H 18 c 35·80, H 21 d 15·40, H 22 a 22·00, H 16 d 50·80, H 17 a 40·50. The relief was completed by 1 p.m.	B.O.M. B.O.M. B.O.M.
	3-2-17		The 138 Machine Gun Company relieved no 1 gun position at E 35 9 30. We placed a gun at H23 c 63·05 for Anti-Aircraft work. We now have three sections in line, relieving before as last only two complete sections - at the time one section a half at Pommier & half between a Bienvillers to prepare work etc.	B.O.M.
	5-2-17		2nd Lieut Baker W.B. & 35174 Pte Sunby C. arrived as reinforcement from the Base.	B.O.M.

Army Form C. 2118.

WAR DIARY
or
INTELLIGENCE SUMMARY

(Erase heading not required.)

137 Bn Machine Gun Coy.

Place	Date	Hour	Summary of Events and Information	Remarks and references to Appendices
POMMIER	8-2-17		Ref MAP FOURQUIVILLERS 57.d.N.S 1/10000 RANSART S.E. 1/10000 Artillery bombarded enemy trenches about MONCHY 11.30 a.m. Got away to a front line from guns at 6 Battery Hospital. Track N 29 b.1.d Road E 5b 10.60. Sunken Road E 6a 50.00 to E 6a 35.15 Cemetery + Rd E S11 9.7. MONCHY Capt Machine Gun Officers went into Sector of the line.	BM
	12-2-17		The following other ranks reported as temp absent from the Raid. 70519 Pte Castledine E 68432 " Vincent N. 57842 " Whitwood J. 68430 " Watters A.W.	BM
	16-2-17		Stamber Horns were sounded in the trenches & also on far back as Pommier. All ranks stood to and Post Respirators on. It appears that it was sent over from Scar Chill on our Right which slightly affected our own + friends. We had no casualties.	BM

2449 Wt. W14957/M90 750,000 1/16 J.B.C. & A. Forms/C.2118/12.

Army Form C. 2118.

WAR DIARY
or
INTELLIGENCE SUMMARY

(Erase heading not required.)

1/7 Bn. Machine Gun Co

Instructions regarding War Diaries and Intelligence Summaries are contained in F. S. Regs., Part II. and the Staff Manual respectively. Title Pages will be prepared in manuscript.

Place	Date	Hour	Summary of Events and Information	Remarks and references to Appendices
POMMIER	16-2-17		Ref MAP FONQUEVILLERS 57d N.E. RANSART 51c S.E. 1/10000 Seven enemy aeroplanes attempted to cross our lines but were headed back by our Anti-aircraft guns & our Stokes Guns.	ßM
	18-2-17		137 Rounds taken over half 138 Brigade front. One gun jam in lectation	ßM
	19-2-17		57842 Pte Whitworth T. evacuated to Hospital.	ßM
	21-2-17		The following reported as reinforcements from the Base 81276 Pte Hutchinson S.E. — 21835 . Kirkham J.	ßM
	26-2-17		2 Officers & 40 O.R.s 1/5 North Stafford Regt raided the enemy's trenches at E5a 2000 at 1.55 a.m this morning. Two prisoners were captured & a dug out destroyed. In connection with the raid we had two guns firing as follows No 9 from N27 c 80.25 target E5 &5 & E5.6 v 8 No 11 from N 21 d 61.90 target F 6 a 20.30 Each gun fired 1250 rounds. Times of fire were 10 pm 25/2/17 & 1.55 a.m. 26/2/17	ßM

Army Form C. 2118.

WAR DIARY
or
INTELLIGENCE SUMMARY

(Erase heading not required.)

137 Machine Gun Co

Place	Date	Hour	Summary of Events and Information	Remarks and references to Appendices
Pommier	18.2.17		Ref Map FONQUEVILLERS 57dNE 1/10000 Ransart 51c S.E. 1/10000 Our guns have been firing intense and rapid bursts on enemy's roads, tracks, dumps, HQ's etc + also on likely movement on rear night on far in the rear.	BM O.R[?] i/c 137 Machine Gun Company

WAR DIARY or INTELLIGENCE SUMMARY

Army Form C. 2118.

Vol 14 134th Machine Gun Coy

Place	Date	Hour	Summary of Events and Information	Remarks and references to Appendices
POMMIER	1-3-17	MAP FONQUEVILLERS 57d N.E 1/40000	Enemy's Artillery & Trench Mortars very active. Wire was sun [being] cut in during the morning by the enemy. We are informed that 2nd Lts Steele & B.S. Lee have joined "B" Machine Gun Company 24/1/17. Also that N.C.O. Lee has been posted to 236th Machine Gun Company 3/1/17. Three officers are available to stand off the attack.	B.M. B.M.
	3-3-17		We evacuated positions at E.u.a.70.31.1 & took over the following positions from 138 Machine Gun Company. Relief completed by 12 noon. E.u.c. 45.10 E.10.b. 40.60 E.9.d. 80.75 E.3d. 35.47	B.M.
	5-3-17		In compliance with orders from Division & in account of the movement of the enemy on our Right, we have increased our Lewis Fire, hering both day & night in order to harass & annoy the enemy as much as possible. The following is a list of the principle targets engaged:—	B.M.

Army Form C. 2118.

WAR DIARY
or
INTELLIGENCE SUMMARY

(Erase heading not required.)

13th M. Machine Gun Coy.

Instructions regarding War Diaries and Intelligence Summaries are contained in F.S. Regs., Part II. and the Staff Manual respectively. Title Pages will be prepared in manuscript.

Place	Date	Hour	Summary of Events and Information	Remarks and references to Appendices
Ref. Map FONQUEVILLERS 57 d N.E. 1/10000			RANSART 51 c S.E. 1/10000	
	5-3-17		1. Road & Trench Junction & Quarry. F7a	
			2. Sunken Roads W30a & W30b	
			3. Road W30d	
			4. Brien Graben, Kirchhof Graben Trench and Sunken Road E6	
			5. Road Junction E5b1.6 & E6a1.3	
			6. Area around Monchy Church	
			7. E. of Monchy E6a1.3 & E6a4.8	
			8. Cemetery Cross Roads E5d 9.9	
			9. Road Junction E5b 5.1	BDM
			21848 Sergt Dyke N.G. proceeded to Cadet School England & is struck off the strength. (Auth. W.O. letter No 100/M.G./81. 18-2-17	BDM
	6-3-17		The following positions were taken over by 9th Machine Gun Company attached to 173 Brigade. The relief was completed by 3 p.m.	

WAR DIARY or INTELLIGENCE SUMMARY

Army Form C. 2118.

134 Machine Gun Co.

Place	Date	Hour	Summary of Events and Information	Remarks and references to Appendices
POMMIER	6-3-17		Ref Map FONQUEVILLERS 57d N.E. 1/10000 RANSART 51 c S.E. 1/10000 Ref Map FONQUEVILLERS N.28.c.92.40, N.23.c.46.35, N.23.d.05.10, N.18.c.40.87, N.21.d.18.33, N.22.a.22.07, N.17.a.55.45. Enemy is making very frequent use of gas shells lately & employs them chiefly - firing at our roads & tracks to and from Hebuterne. The Pommier positions were taken over by 9th Machine Gun Coy. + the relief completed by 5.30 p.m. 2/Lt Thomson H. Evacuated to hospital. The Headquarters of 134 Coy. came in at Pommier for the night.	BGU BGU BGU BGU
	7-3-17		7/8 March. 5/23942. Pte Watmore T. reported sick unfit duty. The Company paraded at 8 a.m. Fighting Order - taken over fresh. By 8.15 a.m. we moved off at 8.25 a.m. (Under Brigade Order) to GRENAS. The route taken was St Amand, Gaudiempré, Pas, Grenas & we arrived at the above place at 11.30 a.m. Dinner was ready by 2.30 p.m & the men spent the remainder of the day resting.	BGU BGU BGU Ref Map LENS 11 1/100000 BGU
GRENAS	9-3-17		The morning was chiefly spent in examining the guns, Spare Parts Cases, Mens kit inspection. Drill - Gun Drill - Aiming & Gun Drill	

Army Form C. 2118.

WAR DIARY
or
INTELLIGENCE SUMMARY
(Erase heading not required.)

137 Machine Gun Coy

Place	Date	Hour	Summary of Events and Information	Remarks and references to Appendices
GRENAS	9-3-17		MAP LENS 1/100000 Sheet RETTEMOY FARM 1/40000 and Tactical Scheme. Afternoon – Football. 2/18/14 Capt Fellows. A. evacuated to C.C.S.	BM BM
	10-3-17		Parade 8.30 a.m. Inspection by Section Officers & talk by C.O. Company Arill + Physical Arill. Afternoon Football. Until with it. 137 Trench Mortar Battery.	BM
	11-3-17		Company paraded ready to march to BAYENCOURT 8.45 a.m. Route taken PAS, HENU, SOUASTRE, BAYENCOURT. Train of mind 12 mm. Rest of the day spent resting.	BM
	13-3-17		Morning spent in advanced Gun drill. Afternoon – Football Match. At 4.30 p.m. Orders were received that we were to attack BUCQUOY GRABEN and Trench mmmy – Front of BUCQUOY mmmy at night Z 2 K. Two of our guns were attached to the front battalion operating the former & 4 guns to 2nd battalion attacking the latter. The nemaing had 6 guns in reserve behind ROSSIGNOL WOOD. The remaining 4 guns were attacking to 2 titles. Zero hour was fixed to be 11.40 p.m. but subsequently postponed to 1 a.m. 14.7	BM

Army Form C. 2118.

WAR DIARY
or
INTELLIGENCE SUMMARY
(Erase heading not required.)

134 Machine Gun Coy.

Instructions regarding War Diaries and Intelligence Summaries are contained in F. S. Regs., Part II. and the Staff Manual respectively. Title Pages will be prepared in manuscript.

Place	Date	Hour	Summary of Events and Information	Remarks and references to Appendices
BAYENCOURT	15-3-17	1 a.m.	SHEET RETTEMOY FARM 1/10000 The attack was launched at 1 a.m. The right Battalion was held up by wire, the left Battalion succeeded in entering the German Trenches but were unable to hold on to them. Owing to destroy of trench the left Battalion withdrew. Our position was not held our guns did not go over. Lewis Guns sent up & at 11 a.m. to fire alarm guns, instead 4 teams moved back to LITTLE BAYENCOURT for 3 hrs, when Lt Halls sent majority down + shot wind + came of men. Our casualties were nil, 1, 32 men were attached to us from 1/6 N. Staffs Regt for carrying purposes + one of them was hit by shrapnel — it was 70501 Pte Goodie H. arrived in reinforcement.	BM BM
	16-3-17		Day spent — resting.	BM
	17-3-17		Day spent — cleaning up guns + materiel. One of our Section of 4 guns detached from the Company + sent to NANNES CAMPS under control of C.O. 1/6 S. Staffords Regt.	BM
			21864 Capt Stanley S. } arrived in reinforcement from the base 82017 Pte Bembridge J. } 82672 Porter C.G. } 21861 Pte Richards C } evacuated to hospital 43265 Pte Robertson J }	BM BM

Army Form C. 2118.

WAR DIARY
or
INTELLIGENCE SUMMARY
(Erase heading not required.)

Instructions regarding War Diaries and Intelligence Summaries are contained in F.S. Regs., Part II. and the Staff Manual respectively. Title Pages will be prepared in manuscript.

B¼ Bn Machine Gun Coy

Place	Date	Hour	Summary of Events and Information	Remarks and references to Appendices
BAYENCOURT	18-3-17		Ref LENS 11 MAP 1/100000 AMIENS 1/100000	
	19-3-17		Move to FONQUEVILLERS via CHATEAU de la HAIE 9 a.m. Detailed section at HANNESCAMPS returned to Company 1 p.m.	BM BM
	20-3-17 21-3-17 22-3-17		Dz 7113 Pte Ryley W transferred to 41st C.C.S. 318743 Cpl Rigby J C.C.S. 311832 Cpl Nightingale 20th C.C.S. BUS-EN-ARTOIS	BM BM BM BM
	23-3-17		Lieut Shaw V.E. arrived as reinforcement from the Base 82434 Pte Hamilton J } 81990 Pte May D } arrived as 81215 Hunt Ca 36671 } Harnett E } reinforcement from the Base	
	24-3-17		Marched to CANTOY	BM
	25-3-17		Marched to VILLERS-BOCAGE	BM
	26-3-17		Entrained at VILLERS-BOCAGE & moved to FERRIERES where we disembarked & marched to RENANCOURT. (2½ kilometres WEST of AMIENS) LIEUT. WOOD C.L. proceeded to England to M. & C.T.C. Passes were given to any men desirous of visiting AMIENS from	BM
	27-3-17		2 p.m. to 8.15 p.m. 2157, Pte Brailsford H. died in Hospital 8629 Pte Reynolds R (attached from 1st/5th S. Staffords) to 50th Pte Gould M, & 811 Pte Ashcroft A. evacuated to C.C.S.	BM BM BM BM

Army Form C. 2118.

WAR DIARY
or
INTELLIGENCE SUMMARY

(Erase heading not required.)

137 Machine Gun Coy.

Place	Date	Hour	Summary of Events and Information	Remarks and references to Appendices
Rd AMIENS	28-3-17	noon	Entrained at BACQUEL STATION at 11.16 p.m.	BRM
	29-3-17		Arrived BERGUETTE STATION at 4.15 p.m. Marched to billets at St. HILAIRE at 6.30 p.m. arriving about 8 p.m.	BM
HAZE	30-3-17		2nd Lieut. Park F.A.K. H.Q. Corps arrived on reinforcement from 1st Army	BM

B R Munn
Lieut
f. O.C. 137 Machine Gun Coy.

Army Form C. 2118.

WAR DIARY or INTELLIGENCE SUMMARY

(Erase heading not required.)

APRIL 1917
137ᵗʰ M.G. COMPANY
SHEET 1
Vol 15

Place	Date	Hour	Summary of Events and Information	Remarks and references to Appendices
St HILAIRE			REF MAP HAZEBROUCK S⁴	
	1-4-17		203230 Pte Davies W.N. admitted to us from 1/5 S.Staff Regt & explain 8619 Pte T Reynolds E. evacuated to No 4 C.C.S. 2/4/17	BEM
	2-4-17		Church Parade 9.30 a.m. 241881 Pte Loder J.N. admitted to us from 1/6 S.Staff Regt & explain 90.	BEM
			Parkin	
	3-4-17		Training 8.30 to 1pm & 2pm to 3.30pm. Fortress, knowledge - of officers	BEM
			Training of small bore Range firing (MGs + Rifles) Physical drill Coy 5.30 to 6 pm	
			Reveille & officers Lecture to officers	
	4-4-17		2777 Sergt Roberts S.T. proceeded to Cadet School England	BEM
			(Authority D.A.G. CD No 46795/12/18/4)	
			Training. Rifle selection of Gun positions. Range firing (M.B. & Rifles)	
			Lectures to officers by Transport officer "Transp" (Horses) Recover of officers ... (Authority A.D.& S. van A.Z. 39/62)	BEM
	5-4-17		9029 Pte Healey J. sent to Base, under age	BEM
			Employed Route March	BEM
	6-4-17		68430 Pte Hollinson A.W. evacuated to WR C.C.S.	BEM
			9056 Pvny S. (R.A.M.C.) attached for Water Cart duty evacuated to WR C.C.S	

Army Form C. 2118.

WAR DIARY
or
INTELLIGENCE SUMMARY
(Erase heading not required.)

April 1917
137th M. Gun Coy
SHEET 2.

Place	Date	Hour	Summary of Events and Information	Remarks and references to Appendices
ST HILAIRE			Ref MAP HAZEBROUCK 1/100000	
	7-4-17		Training as usual. Lecture to Officers 4.45 pm. to 5.30pm "Indirect Fire".	B.M.
	8-4-17		Concert was given by the Company at Chateau (6"9 N.E.) St HILAIRE. Church Parade 10 a.m.	B.M.
	9-4-17		Inspected Rente Morel. The paved Starting Point, Camp Route 300 yards South of E - COTTES at 9.46 a.m. in fine order.	B.M.
	10-4-17		82982 Pte Guiney H.T.] Arrived as reinforcement from the Base 67392 " Golden R. 36868 " Talbot J.E. 10441 " Cornell a.	B.M.
	11-4-17		Every ? man had training as before & at drill. Rehearsing Stoppages. Immediate action. Pit Reproach Drill etc	B.M.
	12-4-17		Moved to BETHUNE via LILLERS & CHOCQUES. Passing starting point (Junction of LILLERS-LIERES ROADS) at 9.5 a.m. Billeted in MONTMORENCY BARRACKS	B.M.
	13-4-17		Through Kit & Gun Inspection in barracks. 35215 6/Cpl Loube C.J. 21726 Pte Mumford W.A. proceeded to BOULOGNE to report to O.C Transportation Troops Depot. Auth A.R. 2 [?] Inf BEF. A.R. 156 H.Q 158/A/4/13	B.M.

Army Form C. 2118.

WAR DIARY
or
INTELLIGENCE SUMMARY

(Erase heading not required.)

137th M. Gun Company. April 1917. Sheet 3

Instructions regarding War Diaries and Intelligence Summaries are contained in F.S. Regs., Part II. and the Staff Manual respectively. Title Pages will be prepared in manuscript.

Place	Date	Hour	Summary of Events and Information	Remarks and references to Appendices
AIRAINES	14/4/17		Church Parade 10 a.m.	B.P.U.
	15/4/17		Tactical Scheme. Company marched to FOURCRUVIC & attacked the STATION	B.P.U.
	16/4/17		Owing to inclemency of weather, training was confined to billets	B.P.U.
	17/4/17		Training + Range firing	B.P.U.
	18/4/17		Marched to LIEVIN arriving at 8 p.m. Commenced relief of 17th M.G. Coy at 11.30 p.m. Relief reported complete at 2 a.m. 19/4/17.	B.P.U.
LIEVIN	19/4/17		One man hit by Resistance gun whilst taking M.G.B. M.G.A (relieving CROOK Strong Point) M.23.8 (relieving CRAZY Strong Point) M.23.A. 8 a.m. Relief between guns at 8th line. Rest in advance of this on nucleus line. Remains of Redoubts west of CROOK + CRAZY are on enemy side of CROOK + CRAZY are on nucleus line. Places M.24.C there is heavy artillery around LIEVIN - LENS Rd and two dill minnies. The enemy here give us a message at LIEVIN. Company HQ is at M.28.A.4.9 Map M186 33·58 NORTH LIEVIN. LENS pretty frequently on ahead are ch Stream Points	

CRESS and CABBY.

Army Form C. 2118.

WAR DIARY or INTELLIGENCE SUMMARY

(Erase heading not required.)

April 1917 137th M Gun Company. Sheet 4

Place	Date	Hour	Summary of Events and Information	Remarks and references to Appendices
LIEVIN	20-4-17		Rif Maj LENS 1/10000 81276 Pte Hutchinson C.E. fatally wounded in face whilst advancing to trenches.	AP11
	21-4-17		21578 Pte Hicks L. "Killed in action". Hostile aeroplane flew over LIEVIN at 6.30 p.m. whilst our two Returns hit his own uncertainty, there were evidently observed as two trucks were dropped any close to H.Q. Latter were put under cover but unusually aeroplane disappeared. Shortn- at his approach the usual battle artillery opened fire. All rattle being used up to 8"	AP11 AP11 AP11
	22-4-17		Artillery active on both sides upon counter battery win. At night two of our guns advanced at M17c 8.4 fired 6000 rds in support cover around HILL 65 - M24d open.	AP11 AP11
	23-4-17		At 4.45 am The 139 Brigade on our RIGHT attacked HILL 65 - M24d. We gave covering fire, vital seven of our guns as follows: Position Target Turn M24c 80.75 M24d 22.70 Zero + M24d 40.30 Zero + 3 M24d 40.30 Zero + 3 M24d 60.40 Zero + 5	AP11

Army Form C. 2118.

WAR DIARY
or
INTELLIGENCE SUMMARY

(Erase heading not required.)

Army Form C. 2118.

137th M[achine] Gun Company Sheet 5

April 1917

Instructions regarding War Diaries and Intelligence Summaries are contained in F.S. Regs., Part II. and the Staff Manual respectively. Title Pages will be prepared in manuscript.

Ref Map LENS 1/10000

Place	Date	Hour	Summary of Events and Information	Remarks and references to Appendices
LIEVIN	22-4-17		No 2 gun — Position M17 d 65.00 — Target M 24 d 40.30 to M 24 d 70.45 — k. M 24 d 90.62 — Time 3 am to 3 am + 5; 3 am + 5 to 3 am + 12	
			No 3 gun — M17 d 60.00 — M 24 d 65.40 to M 24 d 90.85 — k. M 24 d 99.50 — 3 am to 3 am + 5	
			Nos 4, 5, 6, 7 — M17 c 8.4 / M17 c 6.9 — Barrage Fire on Fosse — N19 c 05.20 to M24 d 91.65 — k. N19 c 05.10, N20 a 15.10, N19 b 75.40, N 19 b 70.85 — 3 am to 3 am + 12	

2449 Wt. W14957/M90 750,000 1/16 J.B.C. & A. Forms/C.2118/12.

Army Form C. 2118.

WAR DIARY
or
INTELLIGENCE SUMMARY
(Erase heading not required.)

137th M. Gun Company

April 1917   Sheet 6.

Place	Date	Hour	Summary of Events and Information	Remarks and references to Appendices
LIEVIN	25.4.17		Ref MAP LENS 1/10000	
			The 137 M Groups at Zero (4.45 a.m.) sent out patrols towards the German front ALARM, ABODE Trenches from ADVANCE TRENCH to Churches & Railway at N.13.c.60.86.	
			The idea "front" was unannounced.	
			Our guns fired 30,000 rounds altogether in spite of heavy shelling from the enemy. Two of our guns were hit and another rendered unserviceable.	
			2nd Lieut. Cowley J.D. was wounded on the rim whilst conducting No's 2 & 3 guns machined wire. We had no other casualties.	B.W.
			During the day parties of Germans were seen carrying in their wounded to Lievin.	B.W.
	26.4.17		2nd Lieut Cowley J.D. evacuated to C.C.S.	
			We were relieved of our from M.13.B.55.58 by 139 M.G. Coy. Relief complete by 10 p.m. Advance party of our from i CROOK EVERY ROAD at mew tin	
			The 138 M.G. Coy took over the remainder of our guns, but did not carry on of our position in main LIEVIN – LENS ROAD.	B.W.
			The Company marched back to BULLY-GRENAY by sub sections arrived 3 a.m. 25.4.17 East St Gaten commencing 8.30 p.m.	B.W.

Army Form C. 2118.

WAR DIARY
or
INTELLIGENCE SUMMARY

(Erase heading not required.)

April 1917   137th M. Gun Company

Instructions regarding War Diaries and Intelligence Summaries are contained in F.S. Regs., Part II. and the Staff Manual respectively. Title Pages will be prepared in manuscript.

Place	Date	Hour	Summary of Events and Information	Remarks and references to Appendices
BULLY-GRENAY	25/4/17		Ref. Map LENS 11 1/10000	
			21850 A/Lieut. Evans A. ⎫ Proceeded to BOULOGNE & report to O.C.	BMM
			45551 Pte Davis S.W. ⎬ Transportation Troop Depot & stand by	
			21861 Pte. Richards C. ⎭ though	
			63000 Pte Hunt T.G. ⎫ rejoined the armoured	
			84750 " Sutton H.W. ⎬ Joined as reinforcement from the	BMM
			85360 " Harvest T.J. ⎪ Base	
			84063 " Slatten S.J. ⎭	
	26/4/17		Day spent - Cleaning up + Resting	
			22254 A/Capt Elly F. ⎫	
			66372 Pte Brown F.N. ⎪	
			45059 " Rulleigh R. ⎪	
			86480 " Crow G. ⎬ joined as reinforcement from the BASE	BMM
			68447 " Ray S. ⎪	
			86358 " Connell G.B. ⎪	
			86268 " Bonigaint F. ⎪	
			82017 " Bainbridge J. ⎭	
	27/4/17		rejoined from Hospital	BMM
			Company Drill, Gun Drill, Physical Drill + Football	BMM

WAR DIARY 137th Mn Gun Company Sheet 8.
or
INTELLIGENCE SUMMARY

Army Form C. 2118.

April 1917

Ref Map LENS 11 1/10000   LENS EDITION 8th 1/10000

Place	Date	Hour	Summary of Events and Information	Remarks and references to Appendices
BULLY GRENAY	28-4-17		2nd LIEUT. H.E. GORDON arrived as reinforcement from the Base	BM
			3632 Sergt Nicholls G.L.	BM
	29-4-17		21790 Pte Harper F.W. evacuated to No. 22 C.C.S.	BM
			21837 Sergt Clark R. proceeded to BOULOGNE to meet to England in exchange for 3632 Sergt Nicholls G.L. Auth. D.A.G. C.R. No. 14612/2930	BM
			Thirteen men attached in for duty from the Battalions of the Brigade returned to their respective Battalions.	BM
LIEVIN	30-4-17		Company remained by Sections to LIEVIN to relieve 139 M.G. Coy. The following positions were taken over and material completed by 5 p.m.	BM
			M.35a 55.71 Anti-aircraft Posn	
			M.35a 60.72 Firing E - N.E.	
			M.29c 4.1 Firing due EAST	
			M.29c 74.96 Firing S.E.	
			M.23d 90.89 Firing S.S.E.	
			M.23d 92.07 " N.E. or S.E.	
			M.23a 19.83 " NORTH	
			M.23a 7.4 " S.E.	

(Signed) B.R. Watson
O.C. 137 M.G.Coy

E.R.N. 407
1-6-17

H.Q's GLORY

Herewith War Diary of this
Company for Month of May.

E.R. [signature]
Lieut
O.C. 137 M.G. Coy

Army Form C. 2118.

WAR DIARY
or
INTELLIGENCE SUMMARY

137 Machine Gun Coy. No. 1.

Vol 16

(Erase heading not required.)

Instructions regarding War Diaries and Intelligence Summaries are contained in F. S. Regs., Part II. and the Staff Manual respectively. Title Pages will be prepared in manuscript.

Place	Date	Hour	Summary of Events and Information	Remarks and references to Appendices
LIEVIN	1/5/17		Ref LENS 36 c S.W. 1/10000	
			On account of the Brigade Front being intended Northwards to the BULLY GRENAY – LENS RAILWAY inclusive, we took over four more gunpositions of the 133 M.G. Coy. These are situated in fular. M17d 85.00 (CRECY STRONG POINT) M17c 50.13, M17c 85.47. M18c 35.55. Relief was completed by MIDNIGHT.	8ER
			Enemy's Artillery is not nearly so active as at one a week ago. His guns appear to fire from a very great distance & fire an seen twining in LENS each night.	8EU
	2.5.17		One gun at CRAZY STRONG POINT has been moved back to M23a 35.60 with a field of fire E. to SE. Last night one gun at CRAZY was hit by a shell & another gun had to be sent up from by H.Q. to replace it. The enemy frequently bombard this strong point as well as CROON, & it is probable that if he attempted a raid on a large scale he would barrage these two points & consider the ground untilts evacuated. Such	9.0.2.1 reinforcements 1 OR
			The 138 M.G. Coy are moving this gun from M12c 55.16 to one gun at M 18 c 35.55 is being moved to this position to protrain to position the open ground on NORTH SIDE of Railway, a known gun-making place	8EU

WAR DIARY
or
INTELLIGENCE SUMMARY

Army Form C. 2118.

137 Machine Gun Company No. 2.

(Erase heading not required.)

Summary of Events and Information

Place	Date	Hour	Summary of Events and Information	Remarks and references to Appendices
LIEVIN	3-5-17		Ref LENS 36: S.W. 1/10000	
			A Barrage Scheme has now been arranged by which the whole enemy front & communications are swept by M.G. fire from DUSK till DAWN. This of course can only be engaged on this work each night. The method adopted to ensure that the covered elevation and held is by means of two posts placed crosswise on the top & bottom plate elevation & depression respectively, the sides of which kind the elevation, & the top & bottom plate elevation & depression respectively. The barrel casing of the gun is placed strongly against & clamped by standards & clamping a certain amount of ground is assured of being swept. This has proved most satisfactory and to judge by the retaliation we get is most effective.	108 evacuated Sick
			[Sketch: ELEVATION DIRECTION / DEPRESSION DIRECTION / GROUND LEVEL]	
			During the day we have two guns connected for Anti-Aircraft work but the hostile planes are invariably too high for M.G. fire, especially during the fine weather we are experiencing now.	BM
	4-5-17		The following is an extract from 137 Brigade Routine Orders dated 2nd May 1917. "The Brigadier General Commanding must pleasure in recommending the following awards to N.C.Os of this Brigade for gallantry in the Field:"	108 injured by representation

WAR DIARY
or
INTELLIGENCE SUMMARY 137 Machine Gun Company No. 3

(Erase heading not required.)

Army Form C. 2118.

Place	Date	Hour	Summary of Events and Information	Remarks and references to Appendices
LIEVIN	4-5-17		Ref. LENS 36ᵃ S.W. 1/10000	

Military Medal

No. 70497. Capt. G.L. Griffiths 137 Machine Gun Coy.
No. 23415. Capt. H. Knopper 137 Machine Gun Coy.

These two N.C.Os of this Company displayed great courage + coolness in keeping their guns firing, in spite of a heavy barrage being put on their positions when they went going covering fire to the Infantry of 139 Brigade during the attack on HILL 65 at 4.45 a.m. on morning of 23rd April 1917. Capt. Knopper was in charge of only 3 of the 4 guns from enemy's attempt the team was practically flattened and he kept the gun firing without a stoppage. Capt. Griffiths fired 3000 rds in spite of heavy barrage + in spite of 4 gun being covered with earth thrown up by enemy's shells, caused a temporary stoppage on two occasions. If 2 LT Corley who was in charge of the gun + wounded on this occasion repeatedly brought to notice the gallant conduct of this N.C.O.

Enemy Artillery has considerably increased during the last 24 hours + to replies vigorously to our offensive bombardments. He evidently has good observation from the high buildings in LENS. The chimney of FOSSE 14 in N.2.C. appears to be used for this purpose, as pouffs of smoke are frequently

5-5-17

JML

Army Form C. 2118.

WAR DIARY
or
INTELLIGENCE SUMMARY
137 Machine Gun Company No. 4

(Erase heading not required.)

Summary of Events and Information

Place	Date	Hour	Summary of Events and Information	Remarks and references to Appendices
LIEVIN	5/5/17		Ref LENS 36c. S.W. 1/10,000. elected when visible only from this direction.	BM
	6/5/17		Enemy aeroplanes very active & several aircraft took place. One of our machines flying at an altitude of about 500 ft was suddenly attacked by a German machine which was flying at a higher altitude. A spatter of flame appeared to shoot from the petrol tank of our machine & in a few seconds it was on fire. The pilot tried to make a long dive but the machine collapsed in mid-air, & the line broken & the engine fell close to ELECTRIC POWER STATION M.36.a. Four of our machines brought down an enemy machine at about 6 pm M.36.a. Fires still burning in LENS.	1. O.R. Wounded BM
			Hostile heavy gun searched for our 6" Battery situated at about M.28.a 3.5 from 9am to 10am. About 150 shells were put over & although several passed in the vicinity of the guns none hit the guns & none were detonated.	BM
			At 10 pm, the enemy began to shell LIEVIN with guns–shells until 4am. Guns were fell during this time at the rate of about 20 per minute. It is estimated that at least 6000 shells (gas) were fired. Retaliation enabling BM	
			We were informed at 9.30 in the afternoon that the Enemy had been seen concentrating in ABUCOURT TRENCH or had puts of our guns laid on this trench & the vicinity to [?]	

2449 Wt. W14957/M90 750,000 1/16 J.B.C. & A. Forms/C.2118/12

WAR DIARY
or
INTELLIGENCE SUMMARY 137 Machine Gun Coy   No 5

Army Form C. 2118.

(Erase heading not required.)

Place	Date	Hour	Summary of Events and Information	Remarks and references to Appendices
LIEVIN	7-5-17		Shot bursts during the night & until return that if any disturbance resumed to open rapid fire.	B.M.
	8-5-17		At 4 a.m. a combined Artillery & Machine Gun Barrage was placed on ADJACENT TRENCH lasting for about 20 minutes. Enemy retaliation was very weak. Artillery of both sides very quiet today. No aerial activity owing to dull weather.	B.M.
	9-5-17		Weather much brighter & more aerial activity. Two hostile aeroplanes flew over our lines at a height of about 9000 ft. They were turned about by S.A.A. our Machine Guns. We have placed another gun in the line today at M.18.a.00.45. 72. Four accepts might along the front of CRIMSON TRENCH and is also used as an Anti-aircraft gun during the day. We have now 12 guns in the line. In conjunction with an enterprise of the Canadians on our Right we fired from our guns on to Village & Trenches - N.25.d. 7th Canadians attacked a trench WEST of this target & were quite successful, having very light casualties & capturing a few prisoners.	B.M. B.M.
	10-5-17		Enemy Artillery very active all day along the whole front. Enemy	B.M.

Army Form C. 2118.

WAR DIARY
or
INTELLIGENCE SUMMARY

137 Machine Gun Coy.

No. 6.

(Erase heading not required.)

Place	Date	Hour	Summary of Events and Information	Remarks and references to Appendices
LIEVIN	16-5-17		Ref. LENS S.W 36^c 1/10000 aircraft were exceptionally busy crossing & recrossing our lines all day. At 8.30 p.m. the enemy attempted to reoccupy trench taken from them by the Canadian yesterday. Our RIGHT Gun, No.1, opened fire immediately the S.O.S. signal went up, on target Village & trenches N.S.N. The attack was slowly repulsed. Our gun kept up a barrage on this target until 4.30 a.m. The enemy appeared to be very nervous after the attack & on several occasions sent up red flares when our Artillery opened fire. Spent quietly shelling all day by the enemy. 1 O.R. WOUNDED	B.M.M. B.M.M
	11-5-17		We were relieved by 138 M.G. Coy. Relief commenced at 5 p.m. & was complete by 11 p.m. The enemy's artillery was particularly active in our back & communication but we were able to carry through the relief without a casualty. The Company marched by Eastern to BULLY GRENAY on relief.	B.M.M
BULLY-GRENAY	13-5-17		Kit inspection, Bath & Clean clothes for the men.	B.M.M
	14-5-17		Inspection of Gun Material, Gun Retwin, also Company Inspection by C.O. Presentation of Medals to 70497 Cpl G.L. Griffiths and 23715 Cpl. H. Knopper by M.O.C. Division at 6 p.m.	B.M.M. B.M.M

Army Form C. 2118.

WAR DIARY or INTELLIGENCE SUMMARY

137 Machine Gun Coy

No. 7

(Erase heading not required.)

Place	Date	Hour	Summary of Events and Information	Remarks and references to Appendices
BULLY GRENAY	15-5-17 to 18-5-17	Ref. LENS 11 1/10000	LENS S.W. 36c 1/10000. The usual training was carried out during this period, consisting of Company Drill, Gun Drill, Musketry, Bot Respirator Drill and Inspections. Football & Boxing were indulged in during the evenings.	I.D.R. Trenches to Bruisens 16/5/17. ELM.
	19-5-17		We relieved the 139 Machine Gun Company in the LEFT SECTOR of the Divisional front. Relief commenced 5.30 pm and 10 of the guns were relieved during daylight. The remaining Guns were not relieved till dark. Relief complete 12.15 a.m. 2nd LIEUT W.B. RABER sick to England.	ELM.
German Old Front Line 90c 5/17 M10c61.70			Our line is held by a screen of outposts - front of our Front Line which is at main line of resistance. Behind the main line the support line + then the Brigade Reserve line and the Divisional Reserve line. We have three guns in the Front Line, four guns in Support Line, Seven - Brigade Reserve line (MUSIC TRENCH, used chiefly for barrage fire and indirect fire). The remaining Guns are in Reserve at Company HQ. Our chief targets for indirect fire are the LABASSEE - LENS ROAD, CITÉ ST EMILE, CITÉ ST ELIZABETH and ROADS leading out from N14C. The enemy's artillery has, of to now, been inclined to be quiet. There is a good deal of aerial activity and Enemy aeroplanes frequently cross our lines sometimes with M.G. Range.	ELM.

Army Form C. 2118.

WAR DIARY
or
INTELLIGENCE SUMMARY
(Erase heading not required.)

137 Machine Gun Company
No. 8.

Instructions regarding War Diaries and Intelligence Summaries are contained in F.S. Regs., Part II. and the Staff Manual respectively. Title Pages will be prepared in manuscript.

Place	Date	Hour	Summary of Events and Information	Remarks and references to Appendices
M10a 61.70	21-5-17		Ref. LENS S.W. 36° 1/10000 — LOOS 36° N.W. 1/10000	
			We have three guns employed for Anti-Aircraft work from DAWN and although they have met no yet, succeeded in bringing down a German 'plane they have several times driven back machines which attempted to cross our lines.	
			One gun at N16.40.45 is employed every night in keeping open a gap in wire in front of NASHS ALLEY and Lu 30 for succeeded.	BM
			At 6.30 p.m. tonight one of our aeroplanes was brought down EAST of LOOS by four enemy machines. It appeared to land under control and is our own lines.	BM
			Trench mortar is trench guns in the whole front. Much aerial activity on both sides. 1 OR reported after concussion.	BM BM BM
	22-5-17			
	23-5-17		At 7 pm the 1/6 N. Staff Regt attacked NASH ALLEY from N16.00.32 to N16.76.95 with 2 Companies of 1/6 S. Staffs Regt in support. Our artillery barrage opened at Zero and at Zero + ½ minutes our infantry left the trenches & moved forward to attack the objective at Zero + 3½ minutes. The Company placed a Machine Gun ha barrage in connection. Trenches, Junction of Trenches, Roads, Trench Mortar emplacements and likely points behind the objective, commencing from Summit Trench point N16 A 31 A	

WAR DIARY or INTELLIGENCE SUMMARY

Army Form C. 2118.

137 Machine Gun Coy
No. 9

Place	Date	Hour	Summary of Events and Information	Remarks and references to Appendices
M10a b7d & y5c17	2y 5/17	R of LENS. S.W 36b 1/10000	LOON 36 a N.W. 1/10000 Fire along main LABASSEE - LENS ROAD & COMMOTION TRENCH N18c. Formed of six Lewis M.G. teams was placed in NELSON TRENCH & DYNAMITE MAGAZINE and Trench NORTH and SOUTH of RAILWAY - N1d. In addition FOSSE 14 (N.2c) and CITÉ ST. LAURENT were sprinkled with bullets from Zero to Zero + 40 minutes. Also 3 guns fired direct on NASHALEY. (SOUTH of NIBOSOS) + DYNAMITE MAGAZINE from Zero to Zero + 9. In all 33 Machine Guns were engaged which consisted of 18 M Guns of this Coy (including 4 attached from 178 M.G. Coy) 18 " of 118 M.G. Coy on our LEFT 3 " of 138 " on our RIGHT. The orders were for all guns to fire rapid from Zero to Zero + 9 and from Zero to Zero + 40 a slow rate (about 100 rounds per minute) kept up. The guns to remain in main trench for 24 hours after Zero and in event of S.O.S being seen on a telephone call received to open rapid fire. Eleven of our guns were subjected to MUSIC TRENCH (M.5.d and N.11.b) and most a single enemy shell fell near this trench during the whole operations although the trench in only 1900 yds behind the front trench.	

WAR DIARY or INTELLIGENCE SUMMARY

Army Form C. 2118.

137 Machine Gun Coy No 10

Place	Date	Hour	Summary of Events and Information	Remarks and references to Appendices
M.10.a.61.70			Ref MAPS S.W. 36ᵃ 1/10000 36ᶜ N.W 1/10000 57D S.36 N.W. 1/10000	
	24-8-17		Our infantry gained their objective without any serious opposition from the enemy & commenced to consolidate NASH ALLEY and from there to standen trenches from it. Our M. Guns kept up a slow barrage during the whole night.	
	25-8-17		At 11.30 a.m. the enemy opened a very heavy barrage on NASH, NOVEL and NERO TRENCHES with a great proportion of shells in rear of our trenches. The offensive was always of our guns at N.6.d.40.72 surrounding reinforcements from our parapets and had direct hits of NASH (SOMERSET) also. At this time the enemy barrage lifted and he stormed at 12 noon, as this time the enemy barrage lifted and he stormed the enemy leaving HEYLEY Trench to H.16 and to surrounding trenches and he gun not there. The enemy also a LEFT FORM in leaving the trenches and attacked portion of NASH held by us. Owing to smoke and mist by the enemy previous to the attack the troops were only visible at times but our guns caused a great many casualties and drove out this line eventually 1500 the rapid was fired at the advancing troops and the part at the gun position was heavily shelled. When enemy barrage opened at 11.30 a.m. our M.G. troops fired at a slow rate and at 12 noon when our S.O.S. was seen all guns opened rapid fire which was continued until 12.30 p.m.	

WAR DIARY
or
INTELLIGENCE SUMMARY

Army Form C. 2118.

137 Machine Gun Coy
No. 11

Place	Date	Hour	Summary of Events and Information	Remarks and references to Appendices
M13a 6.7.9 (sheet 36c N.W 1/20000)				
	26-5-17	Ref LENS S.W 36c 1/20000 Lens 36c N.W 1/10000	Our troops were forced to evacuate MAISON ALLEY owing and our trench was blown in. Army took over our front 56 ovvo rounds. During night 24/25 on front 47,000 " During Counter attack 25th on front 52,000 " In addition it is estimated that the guns of 18 M.G. Coy and 137 M.G. Coy assisting in front over 300,000 rds.	B.U.
			During the night 25/26 we fired 35,000 rounds on enemy communication trenches, tracks, light railways and side of CITÉ ST AUGUSTE.	B.U.
M16 b 55 g 97 - 5-17			At 15 pm we took over the Battn. H.Q. at M.16 b 55 g 97. 1.O.R. transferred to 164 M.G. Coy Counter-battery work done by west side.	B.U.
	28-5-17		Enemy very quiet. Much Counter-battery work done by both sides.	B.U.
			Enemy artillery active on our forward trenches.	B.U.
M.11 c 18 75	30-5-17		Moved to new Head Quarters at M.11 c 18 75	1.O.R. "Killed in action"
	31-5-17		Total reinforcement for this month 11 O.Rs. (4 from Base 2 from Hospital) Total evacuation for this month { 1 Officer 7 O.Rs. { 2 O.Rs. Wounded { 1 O.Rs. Killed in action { 2 O.Rs. Sick & Injured & evacuated { 2 O.Rs. transferred to Trench Mortar & Trench Mortar B.M. 9 G.N.E.	B.U.

E. R. Linzend
L.O.C. 137 M.G. Coy.

To HQ.
137 Bde

No. 137
MACHINE GUN
COMPANY.
No. B/444
Date 3.7.17

Herewith War Diary of
137th Machine Gun Company for
Month of June 1917

Donnan Henry, Lt.
for OC.
137 M/G Coy

WAR DIARY
or
INTELLIGENCE SUMMARY

(Erase heading not required.)

Army Form C. 2118.

137 M. Gun Company   No 1

Vol 17

Place	Date	Hour	Summary of Events and Information	Remarks and references to Appendices
M1C 18.75 Ref LENS S.W. 36c 1/10000	1-6-17 to 5-6-17		Nothing of importance has happened on our front during this period. No fire was opened from DUSK to DAWN on enemy ROADS, TRACKS and COMMUNICATIONS from at an average about 1500 rds. One machine gun used for anti-aircraft work.	16-17 1 OR Wounded 1 O.R. to Cadet School. England.
	6-6-17		Aerial observation shows that enemy planes are recently seen approaching our M. Gun targets has been prepared them previously. Enemy Artillery very active on our front has not commenced their previously from 9 pm - 6 pm. It is now suspected when they arrived and this properly all the enemy expected our attack today.	7. O.R. reported for instruction 2 Ball 2 O.R. wounded 2nd C.C.S.
	7-6-17		In conjunction with raid of Division of our LEFT in which in support attacked — MUSIC TRENCH we enemy trenches in rear of objective. Zero hour was 12.15 a.m. and from Zero to 12.20 a.m. we fired rapid, keeping up a slow rate barrage of 15 rds per minute throughout the raid. Total rounds fired 12000. Enemy successfully gassed.	2. Ball
	8-6-17		Much Artillery Activity all day. In conjunction with the Barrage on our RIGHT 2 Companies of 1/5 S. Staffs Regt raided NASHALLEY from N1a 97 38 to N1a 7? 95 at 8.30 p.m. In connection with the raid we placed a Vickers Gun Post Barrage	2/Lt H.E. Cannon 7 J.R. wounded

WAR DIARY or INTELLIGENCE SUMMARY

Army Form C. 2118.

137 M. Gun Company No. 2.

Place	Date	Hour	Summary of Events and Information	Remarks and references to Appendices
M11c.18.75	8-6-17		Ref LENS S.W. 36° 1/10000 LOOS 36ᵃ N.W. 1/10000	

on COMMUNICATION TRENCHES, JUNCTIONS of trenches & ROADS, TRENCH MORTAR emplacements and STRONG POINTS behind the objective, commencing from German front line in N31d, drawn along main LABASSEE - LENS RD to COMMOTION TRENCH N8c. Forward of this Road, the Lt G. Guns who played on NELSON TRENCH, DYNAMITE MAGAZINE and trenches N. and S. of RAILWAY - N1d. Twenty-two guns were used for this barrage, including 4 guns of 178 M. Gun Cy attached to us for that purpose and 8 guns of the 18th M. Gun Coy on our LEFT who co-operated but did not...

In addition to above 2 of our guns fired elevated on to NASH ALLEY SOUTH of NETLEY TRENCH

All gun fire opened from Zero to Zero + 9 and from Zero + 9 to + 40 a slow rate barrage of 60 rds per minute was kept up. From Zero + 40 until withdrawal of machine 15 rds per minute were fired and changed to slight bursts of fire of about 10 rds to minute were fired from each Gun. Ten of our Guns were situated in MUSIC TRENCH (M.51d and N11b) about 1900 yards behind the assault position covering the attack of our infantry left on trenches and movement at Zero + 1/2 minutes our infantry left our trenches and movement enters the enemy trench, killing many and capturing 8 prisoners

Army Form C. 2118.

WAR DIARY
or
INTELLIGENCE SUMMARY

137 Machine Gun Company No. 3

(Erase heading not required.)

Place	Date	Hour	Summary of Events and Information	Remarks and references to Appendices
M11c 18.75	8-6-17		Ref LENS S.W. 36ª 1/10000 and LOOS 36ᶜ N.W. 1/10000. and Machine Guns. They did not return until 10 p.m.	B.M.
	9-6-17		Exceptionally quiet	B.M.
	10-6-17			Lt. P. Jeffery invalided to Base Sick
	11-6-17		A Combined Artillery and Machine Gun "Strafe" on enemy roads, Trench, Communications and defences took place along the whole Divisional Front. Bombardments of three phases took place at 3 minute intervals at 10 p.m. to 12.15 a.m. In connection with this we fired 7 guns firing at the rate of 100 rds per minute at and and bombardment. 15,000 rds were fired in all.	B.M.
	12-6-17		About Midday our team at N.1.C. 45.45 consisting of 1 Off/Sgt and 4 men were all killed and the gun and material destroyed by an enemy heavy trench mortar shell. We are not placing another gun there but arrange is to cover the front by No's 5 and 6 guns.	3 O.R. Killed in Action.
	13-6-17		At 10.25 p.m. two Companies of 1/5 N. Staff. Regt. carried out a raid	

Army Form C. 2118.

WAR DIARY
or
INTELLIGENCE SUMMARY
(Erase heading not required.)

137 Machine Gun Company
No. 4.

Place	Date	Hour	Summary of Events and Information	Remarks and references to Appendices
M.I.C. 18.73	14.6.17		Ref LENS S.W 36 c 1/10000	

On NARWAL and CONTRACT trenches between N7a 97.50 and N10.16.16.

The object of the raid was to establish identification and to destroy the enemy's defences and troops.

At Zero hour a special company of the R.E.'s projected burning oil on to DYNAMITE MAGAZINE defences.

The operation was very successful, the machines were turned to return at Zero + 40 minutes but it was put 11.50 pm when the "Horn's" signal was observed. Two prisoners were brought back of very poor physique and suspiciously stripped and it is estimated that the enemy lost about 50 of the enemy wounded or killed by shelling.

Our Machine Guns assisted by placing a hot barrage round the objective 9 guns being used for this purpose. In addition our fire from N7a 25.40 traversed and shelved fire on to enemy trench N10.58.30 to N10.88.38.

Also 18" M.G. Co on our LEFT assisted and 2 M.G. Co.

The principle targets for the barrage fire were Tunnel Junctions, Front Line, in flanks of Objective, Road Junctions, Roads and streets and C.T.'s.

Total number of Rounds fired by our guns was 28000. Rate of fire was

WAR DIARY or INTELLIGENCE SUMMARY

Army Form C. 2118.

137 Machine Gun Company No. 5

Place	Date	Hour	Summary of Events and Information	Remarks and references to Appendices
M.18.75 Ref LENS 1/20,000 S.W. 36° 1/10000	14.6.17 to		Zero + 10 minutes from Zero + 75 minutes was seen at barrage rate (60 rds per minute) S.O. of the guns were kept on target all night. Firing shot burst at intervals.	2/Lt B. KIDD reinforcement from Base.
	15.6.17		We were relieved by the 189 M. Gun Company. Relief was completed by 11.40 pm without casualties. Company marched to BULLY GRENAY by Sub Sections. This has been the longest tour the Company has ever served & being formed. From 19th April until today we have fired 170[?] guns continuously in the line from 1 claim in 4 appreciably two spots.	
BULLY GRENAY M2 B.3.	16.6.17 to 21.6.17		The usual training was carried out during this period, consisting of Company Drill, Inspection of Kit & Gun Material, Gun Drill, Box Respirator Drill & Lectures. Also two animal Tactical Schemes & a demonstration of indirect fire on a 2000 yd range. Bath going to the line again Company Sports were organised & a Concert given by Officers & men. On the 13th inst. we competed in the 1st Corps Stand Shoot establishing a record & winning G.S. Waggon.	2/Lt L. DRISCOLL reinforcement from 178 M.G.Coy. 12 R returned from C.C.S. Sch.
LIEVIN M28d 70.31	22.6.17		We relieved the 138th Machine Gun Coy in the RIGHT SECTOR of the Divisional Front. Relief commenced at 3 pm and 12 of the guns were relieved during daylight.	7.6.17 10 R wounded to C.C.S. Sch. 19.6.17 1 OR wounded to C.C.S. Sch.

Army Form C. 2118.

WAR DIARY
or
INTELLIGENCE SUMMARY

(Erase heading not required.)

137 Machine Gun Coy

No. 6

Place	Date	Hour	Summary of Events and Information	Remarks and references to Appendices
M.28.D.78.31. LIEVIN	22.6.17		Ref. LENS 11 1/10,000. The remaining four guns were not relieved till dark. Relief complete 12.15 a.m.	4 O.R. transferred to L Coy from 138 L M.G. Coy.
	23.6.17		Throughout the day & night the enemy was extremely quiet on the whole front.	3 O.R. reinforcements.
	24.6.17		Ref. LENS S.W. 36c 1/10,000. Much artillery activity during the day. At 9.30 p.m. the 46 (South Staffs) Regt. attacked the enemy's first & second lines, AHEAD and ADMIRAL TRENCHES and to consolidate a line to run along BOOT TRENCH, thence to M.30.6.5.4. to M.30.B. 35.93 to M.24.d. 22.20 the attack being made from South to North. Two companies made the attack with one Company in support and one Company in Reserve. Our Artillery Barrage opened at 2 a.m. and at 2 hr + 2 minutes infantry also assembled at M.30 central left for their objectives. This Company placed a machine gun barrage with 12 guns from the CITE JEANNE d'ARC on HILL 65 East of the road running from M.24.d. 40.30 to M.24.d. 53.00. A barrage was also placed on the enemy's main front line trenches ABODE, ADULT, ADJACENT and ALMANAC Trenches. 16 machine guns were employed altogether. 16 Machine Guns were employed attack consisted of :- 4 attached from 173rd Bde 3 divisional 12 this Coy 19 S.A.A. This guns opened fire at 2 a.m. & continued firing at rate of 185 rds per minute until 2 a.m. + 20 & from 2 a.m. + 20 to 2 a.m. + 40 at 60 rds per minute. Short bursts were kept up during the night to lack of fire incoming towards dawn.	1 N.R. Transferred to B Coy from pattern Inf. depot Boulogne.

Army Form C. 2118.

WAR DIARY
or
INTELLIGENCE SUMMARY
(Erase heading not required.)

137 Machine Gun Coy No 7

Place	Date	Hour	Summary of Events and Information	Remarks and references to Appendices
M10D.78.31 LIEVIN	24.6.17		Ref: LENS 11 1/10,000 and LENS S.W. 36c 1/1000 On information being received that our troops were in AGNES Trench on frontage were lifted to a line running from M30b 95.70 to N25a 3.1. In all 39,000 rounds were fired. In addition to the Barrage fire, 2 guns were detailed on a line at N30a 20.75 going direct enfilading fire into Zorts & also on Trench JUNCTION of AHEAD and AGNES. A gun at M24a 70.50 and also at M24 0.5.80 were laid in readiness for anti Tank. Our 3 guns fired all this Operation with little opposition & the captured trench was immediately consolidated. 1 Prisoner was taken & so many of the enemy killed, the rest of them during a bolt from our advance.	A1
	25.6.17		Situation very quiet. Arial activity.	
	26.6.17		Two of our guns fired from dusk till dawn on the enemy wire of ADSACEN and ADJUNCT Trenches to prevent him repairing the gaps cut by Artillery & much counter battery work by the enemy throughout the day.	1 O.R. evacuated to C.C.S. Sick
	27.6.17		Enemy very active & much counter battery work being had, close to our H.Q in which the stay hit 8 men, 3 being killed & 3 wounded through one of the armour	3 O.R. killed in action. 2 O.R. wounded in action.

WAR DIARY or INTELLIGENCE SUMMARY

(Erase heading not required.)

Army Form C. 2118.

137 Machine Gun Coy.   No. 8

Place	Date	Hour	Summary of Events and Information	Remarks and references to Appendices
Ref. LENS 11 1/40,000				
M.80 78½	27.6.17		Heavy shells bursting close in the near dug out which was a direct old enemy gun pit with tunnel attached to dug out.	10 R. casualties
LIEVIN				5 C.C.S. Sub
				DI
	28.4.17		At 2 a.m. on 28th from the Battalion of the 6th N.F. Staff Regt attacked & captured enemy trenches ABODE and ADULT from LENS-LIEVIN ROAD inclusive to ADRIF (Exclusive) and ½ South Staff Regt attacked and captured ADJACENT of to ADRIFT (inclusive) in conjunction with the above the Company placed a Barrage with 8 guns & 4 guns allotted from K.17.b.5.c.9. about N.19.b. 80.40 to N.19.b. 99.10 to N.20.a. 10.20 to N.20.a. 20.00 N.20.a. 15.95 to N.20.c. 15.75. In addition to This guns the others were placed under the command of ½ S. Staff Regt & two others attached to the ½ North Staff plus other guns remained in reserve. The two guns attached to the ½ South Staff went over with K.3. Wave in rear of great attempts Barbara behind the funk line guarding the left flank. The other two (attached to N.Staff) were kept in reserve to go over the unmanaged in position Later they had good fields of fire at the retreating of the Battalion. During the operation the 12 Barrage Guns fired 20,000 rounds.	DI

WAR DIARY
or
INTELLIGENCE SUMMARY.
(Erase heading not required.)

Army Form C. 2118.

137 Machine Gun Coy

No. 9

Place	Date	Hour	Summary of Events and Information	Remarks and references to Appendices
LIEVIN	26.6.17	11 p/1000	LENS S.W. 36c 1/10000 Throughout the day we were prepared for a heavy counter-attack by the enemy which did not take place.	
M.28.a.7.5.3	30.6.17		In cooperation with a Sussex division carried out by the 139th Infantry Bde on our left the North Staffs attacked & captured a block of houses at M.9.a. 60.50 and AGUE Trench Block on the LIEVIN-LENS Road at M.19.b. 60.50 inclusive. Z.n.6. Section was on C.2.7.b.7 m.m. during the above action we had 7 guns laid on a barrage S.O.S. line from M.20.a. 25.55 to M.20.c. 30.80 and M.20.c. 30.80 and four guns attached from the 170th Cy were laid on S.O.S. line at N.13.c. 75.30 to N.14.c. 10.97 we had no counter to fire.	1 O.R. Wounded 2 O.R. Wounded
	30.6.17		Total Reinforcement for the month 2 officers 10 O.R. Total Wounded 1 officer 7 O.R. Total Killed 10 O.R. To Cadre School English 1 O.R. Evacuated to Base 1 gun To sick to Hospital & evacuated 8 O.R. Transferred to Trench Mortar Battery 10 O.R.	1 from Hospital

Norman Harvey Lt.
O.C. 137 M.G. Coy.

A6945 Wt. W14422/M1160 35,000 12/16 D.D.&L. Forms/C/2118/14.

No. 137
MACHINE GUN
COMPANY.
No. B.313
Date. 1 8 17

To HQ
137 Bde

Herewith War Diary of
137th Machine Gun Company
for the Month of July 1917

C Cadbit-Adams
Major
OC
137 M.G.Coy

WAR DIARY
or
INTELLIGENCE SUMMARY.
(Erase heading not required.)

Army Form C. 2118.

137 Machine Gun Coy
No. 1

Vol I B

Place	Date	Hour	Summary of Events and Information	Remarks and references to Appendices
LIEVIN	1.7.17		Ref LENS S.N. 36C 1/10,000 LENS N 1/10,000 N. of LENS S.I.	
M18a 78.31			The 46th Division attacked on a Two Brigade front to secure the line from SOUCHEZ RIVER at N26b 8.6 to N20c 0.2, ACONITE TRENCH and ALOOF TRENCH both to N13a 9.5.65. This line will form up to an original front line by COLLEGE, CORNWALL and COMBAT TRENCHES. This Brigade frontage is from Road running E.N.E. from M24d.74 to LIEVIN – LENS Road both inclusive.	
			The attack was carried out by the 1/5 North Staff and 1/5 South Staff in Suffolk. In conjunction with the above this Company placed a Barrage on N20a & N20c with 8 guns. T 2 other guns fired on NORTH side of Ry. Embankment giving enfilade fire on N13d.30.80 to N13d.99.13. A total of 21,000 rds were fired. Zero hour 2:47 a.m. Our Infantry were successful in gaining their objectives & proceeded to consolidate, but the LEFT Brigade had some slight difficulty & the enemy counter attacked about 7 am. & succeeded in driving him out.	
			During their operation fire from all of this company were placed at the disposal of 1/5 North Staff Regt. but the risk of our catching up their patrols in the assembly trenches & were resorted to for defensive purposes against a counter attack.	

Army Form C. 2118.

WAR DIARY
or
INTELLIGENCE SUMMARY
(Erase heading not required.)

137th Machine Gun Coy
No. 2

Place	Date	Hour	Summary of Events and Information	Remarks and references to Appendices
			Ref: LENS S.N. 36c 1/10,000	
LIEVIN M.18.d.78.31	1.7.17		Ref: LENS 11 1/10,000	
			In addition to the big attack at night another minor operation was carried out by this Division in order to secure our right flank which had not got all the intended objective on the 1st inst. the 139th Bde being unsuccessful on our left. In this operation the 1/5 Scot Rifle attacked the enemy in N.19.b. & taken the area between LIEVIN-LENS and ANGRES-LENS Road (inclusive) up to ACONITE TRENCH & to consolidate. Zero hour was 11 pm. This attack was carried out under the help of artillery barrage. Our guns remained laid on their S.O.S. lines but did not fire excepting two guns which fired on N.13.d. 30.50 & N.13.d. 99.13 continuously throughout the night.	AJ
	2.7.17		The Company was relieved in the trenches by K. & L. Canadian Machine Gun Coy relief commencing at 10.30 pm & was completed by 1 am. The relieving Company having carried hand-guns On relief the Company marched by sections to BULLY GRENAY.	AJ
REVEILLON V.26.d.30.35	3.7.17		The Company entrained at BULLY GRENAY at 2 pm & proceeded to ALLOUAGNE, afterwards marching to our billets at REVEILLON	10R from H/qrs AJ

WAR DIARY
or
INTELLIGENCE SUMMARY

(Erase heading not required.)

Army Form C. 2118.

137th Machine Gun Coy.
No. 3

Instructions regarding War Diaries and Intelligence Summaries are contained in F.S. Regs., Part II. and the Staff Manual respectively. Title pages will be prepared in manuscript.

Place	Date	Hour	Summary of Events and Information	Remarks and references to Appendices
REVEILLON	4/7/17		This day was spent cleaning guns, kit &c. K.K. inspection company of kit & all deficiencies	LD 1 OR reported off evacuation
V26d 30.35			1 invincible returned	
	5/7/17		Training of Company commenced, consisting of Coy. Drill, Rifle Exercises & Physical Drill. Cleaning of all Coy's ammunition. Repairs.	2 OR returned from Hospital
	6/7/17		Company Drill & Route March. Praker in Gun "Standard Tests" Pay.	
	7/7/17		Company Inspection & Gun Drill &c. Lectures to Officers	
	8/7/17		Ceremonial Church Parade cancelled owing to wet weather. Gun Rotor Inspection.	
	9/7/17		Usual training of Company. Physical Training, Coy. Drill. On the Range firing of Table 1c. Praker of Gunn in Open Warfare. Lectures to N.C.O's	1 OR admitted to Hospital 1 OR to Hospital
	"		Recruits from E.O. & to Section Coy Section Officer	2 OR recruits to Hospital
	13/7/17			1 OR evacuated to Hospital

WAR DIARY
INTELLIGENCE SUMMARY
(Erase heading not required.)

Army Form C. 2118.

137th Machine Gun Coy
No. 4.

Place	Date	Hour	Summary of Events and Information	Remarks and references to Appendices
REVEILLON	11/7/17		Ceremonial Church Parade & Presentation to the undermentioned NCO's of the Military Medal by the 1st Army Commander.	10R returned from Hospital
R2nd	30.35		Sgt Paul H.	
			Cpl Ellis A.N. Bth for gallantry in the field on the 28th June during the attack on Hill 65.	
			Sgt Maynard awarded the Military Medal for the same attack being in charge of the two teams that went over.	L/NCO
	15.7.17		General Training of the Company. Routine Ceremonial Drill.	
	16.7.17		Company Drill with Limbers. Inspection of Transport by G.O.C. Division. Very satisfactory. 8 OR Dispatched from 71 M.G.Cy.	15/7 1 OR rejoined from hospital.
	17.7.17		Tactical Scheme for Section Leaders in the afternoon.	7/7 10R to hospital
	18.7.17		Brigade Ceremonial Inspection by G.O.C. Division. The Coy being congratulated on their good turn out. Cricket in the afternoon.	10R wounded to C.C.S 59
	19.7.17		Gun Drill. Buckbum Limited Drill. Revolver Practice Elementary.	

WAR DIARY or INTELLIGENCE SUMMARY

Army Form C. 2118.

137 Canadian Gun Coy   No 5

Place	Date	Hour	Summary of Events and Information	Remarks and references to Appendices
REVEILLON	20.7.17		Company Bath, Range Practice, Register Shoots, Physical Training.	10R recruits 5 Hospital = 4 syph.
Motor Rly 30.38 K			Gas Store & practice of Gun Drill with Gas Helmets worn. Tactical Schemes.	21/7 1.0R insufficient
	24.7.17		Packing of trenches for trench patrols and reliefs. Lectures to N.C.O.'s. Evident	
			Sport. Coy Concert night of 24th inst.	22/7 1.0R recruits 5 Hospital
				23/7 10R report for recruits
	25.7.17		Company moved from REVEILLON T wood to DROUVIN. 8am	A1. 24/7 9, 10R 12 Hospital
DROUVIN	26.7.17		Continued training of Company. Gun drill, Buckman, Range & Barrage Schemes.	A1. 3 17/7 10R report for recruits
Motor Rly			Lectures. Cricket, Riding lines for Officers.	127/7 10R report for recruits
36 B. N.E.	30.7.17			A1. 29/7 10R report for recruits & men 1
K 34 C.2				
	31.7.17		Tactical Scheme combined with march in rear Reptients at night.	
			Total Reinforcements for month. 31 Sick & Hospital 8	
			Total Wounded Nil Returned from Hospital 11	
			Total Killed Nil Casualties Nil	
			Evacuated to Base Nil	

Donovan Harvey Lt.
O.C. 137 M.G. Coy

WAR DIARY
or
INTELLIGENCE SUMMARY

(Erase heading not required.)

Army Form C. 2118.

137 Machine Gun Coy

No. 1

Place	Date	Hour	Summary of Events and Information	Remarks and references to Appendices
			MAP. 36 c N.E. 1/20,000. (BETHUNE)	01/19
DROUVIN	1.8.17		Packing of stores, preparation for moving to the trenches.	
K 36 6.2			Testy of Box Respirators in Gas Chambers. Commenced Musketry for Innoculation of Recruits, on respirators in Gas Coy. Sgt Hayward & No 21775 Sgt Banning returned from the Attack on LENS on 28.6.17. The Sgt being the Section Sgt acted with credit and when going over the top any to effect.	+0% Recruit 4% innoculation
	2.8.17		Relief of 138 M.G. Coy postponed being ordered by [?]	
	3.8.17		Coy marched to MAZINGARBE to relieve the 138th Machine Gun Coy in the line HULLUCH SECTOR leaving DROUVIN at 9.45am. All Gun Positions were relieved by a strength of 8 howi. Leaving DROUVIN during daylight under very bad weather conditions. The enemy shelled very severely 5pm during daylight under very bad weather conditions.	
G.3 6 3.0	4.8.17		Nothing of importance has happened on our front during the past 4 hours. Weather condition very bad. The fight and night are with fire from our from in the enemy Man R's, Truck R Chief communication Trenches. Enemy shelled about 6000 rats for night. Enemy arrived not any active.	10 R [Hosp]L 137 10 R & [Hospital] 8 3/7 1.0.R. & Hosp.
Blc N.N 6?				
	9.8.17		On 7th Inst. The enemy shelled our Trench line & Karinf with gas shells of about 13 minutes.	

WAR DIARY or INTELLIGENCE SUMMARY

Army Form C. 2118.

137 Infantry Brigade
No. 2

(Erase heading not required.)

Instructions regarding War Diaries and Intelligence Summaries are contained in F. S. Regs., Part II. and the Staff Manual respectively. Title pages will be prepared in manuscript.

Place	Date	Hour	Summary of Events and Information	Remarks and references to Appendices
Trenches	9.8.17		MAP 36.B NE 1/20,000 (BETHUNE) 36.c NW 1/20,000 Observation Balloon N.W. of HULLUCH in vicinity of BAUVIN brought down enemy aeroplane by anti aircraft fire, enemy aeroplane at 19.35 am. K aeroplane shot	
G.23.b.3.8			down MAZINGARBE & flying only a few yards above ground made straight for balloon	"J" 1/7 W. 12th HLI
36.c NW "J" from	10.8.17		& fetched it down in flames. The observer sitting to his parachute. Nothing of importance has occurred on our front. Trenches changed over	
	11		The period each night with few guns on the Enemy's Gun Roads, Trenches and chief communication trenches, firing about 600 rounds per night.	"J" 2/7 W. C. HLI "J" 2/7 1/08 from HLI in England.
	12.8.17			
	13.8.17		In connection with 139 Brigade Raid at H.1.30, 9 of our guns fired on enemy's Roads, communication trenches a.c. Total rounds fired 27,000. Hostile aircraft were active. W. engaging our heavier. On anti aircraft fire.	"J" 1/08 "J" H/L/X
	14.8.17		During the night few of our guns fired on enemy's tracks, chief communication trenches a.c. rounds fired 5000. Hostile aeroplanes active during the evening.	"J" 1/08 from "J" C.C.S.

A6945 Wt. W14422/M160 35,000 12/16 D. D. & L. Forms/C./2118/14.

WAR DIARY or INTELLIGENCE SUMMARY

(Erase heading not required.)

Army Form C. 2118.

137 Machine Gun Coy.
No 3

Place	Date	Hour	Summary of Events and Information	Remarks and references to Appendices
Trenches G.23.b.3.3 36cNW 1/20000	15/8/17		MAP 36B N.E. 1/20000 (BETHUNE) 36c N.W. 1/20000 At 4.25 a.m. the Canadian Division on our RIGHT attacked the enemy and captured HILL 70 N.W. of LENS. All objectives were held against repeated counter-attacks. In connection with these operations four of our guns barraged on a line from H.27.d.05.98 to N.26.b.58.10 from Zero +30 to Zero +130 and then acted by by S.O.S. signal. At 11.30 a.m. enemy troops, at least 3000 strong, were seen advancing in extended formation from the direction of WINGLES to the BOIS HUGO. It was most difficult to carry out an operation on any increased scale to the eye but importunately for them 8 of our M Gunners spotted them and elevated up getting what is now a direct target, opened rapid fire on the loads which they caught almost in enfilade and created havoc and destruction amongst them. These troops had evidently been brought up to WINGLES and sent across the BOIS HUGO to reinforce the troops in front of the Canadians and to execute a counter attack on them.	

A6945 Wt. W11427/M1160 35,000 12/16 D.D. & L. Forms/C./2118/14.

WAR DIARY
or
INTELLIGENCE SUMMARY.
(Erase heading not required.)

137 Machine Gun Cy. Army Form C. 2118.

No. 4.

Place	Date	Hour	Summary of Events and Information	Remarks and references to Appendices
H.Q.s	15.8.17		Ref. Map 36 c N.W. 1/20000 — the new	
G.23.6.3.B			There was great activity throughout the day. at about 7.30 p.m one of our M. Gun fired at a hostile plane with tracer bullets and about 10 rounds afterwards the plane was seen to crash to the ground.	2. O.R.s Wounded
			is own lines the wings having come away from the body of the machine meanwhile. It is probable that the M.G. bullets broke the stays of the wings and this deform of the gun expedited the wings from the body.	10 R. hand perdo
			Enemy counter-attacked Canadians yesterday at 8.55 p.m. but were repulsed	S.R.U
	16-8-17	At 8.30 p.m	Canadian S.O.S was seen and our front gunner laid on Canadian S.O.S. barrage lines fired 10.000 rds.	
			A raid was carried out on the front of the Brigade on my LEFT by a Bath. of 138 Bde. and S.O.s was fired in protection on the flanks of the raid raided and at enemy M.G.s. 17000 rds were fired	2.OR & Mple
			He also fired 2.000 rds on HOLLEBUCH MENIN ROAD— harassing fire	1 OR 4 Base Syn
		At 8 p.m our two Bu't aircraft M.Gs repeatedly turned enemy planes back	S.R.U

Army Form C. 2118.

WAR DIARY
or
INTELLIGENCE SUMMARY.
(Erase heading not required.)

137 M. Gun Coy.
No. 5.

Instructions regarding War Diaries and Intelligence Summaries are contained in F. S. Regs., Part II. and the Staff Manual respectively. Title pages will be prepared in manuscript.

Place	Date	Hour	Summary of Events and Information	Remarks and references to Appendices
H.Qs. G.23.b.3.	17-8-17	Ref Map 36c N.W. 1/20000	Champion S.O.S. came at 11.30 p.m. and all of our guns opened fire on Canadian S.O.S. Barrage lines, in addition to other from a MG on target.	6
	18-8-17		Our LEFT SECTOR opened fire on LEFT FLANK of the Canadian Corps at 1.45 a.m. and 3.45 a.m. The above Canadian S.O.S. was again sent at 1.45 a.m. and 3.45 a.m. The enemy guns opened fire on our positions being ranged 7800 yds. The enemy counter attacked at 1.45 a.m. and 3.45 a.m. were prepared by firing for shells and our barrage was obliged to send but inspiration stall firing the guns.	Barrage jammed
				6.M.M
	18-8-17		Enemy enemy planes were seen to attack about 6 p.m. between HOUFFEN and WINGLES. The fight good. 1 to 2 of enemy planes between Sein and S.45 a.m. this morning.	2 O.R.s slightly gassed
				6.M.M
	18-8-17 to 28-8-17		In compliance with Divisional Order G.727/68 one less period 3 of guns August G.56.2.5.60, Butt. H.Q. G.56.b.5.9.9.1. Temporary Terminus G.56.21.87. These 3 guns have fired about 10000 rds each night to the great annoyance of the enemy who have responded for	20.7, 30.6 Rifle. 2. O. R.s wounded 22 – 8 – 3
			these mid and artillery and M.G.	22-7, 19R.K. Hazard

A6945 Wt. W14422/M1160 35,000 12/16 D. D. & L. Forms/C./2118/14.

Army Form C. 2118.

137 M. Gun Coy
No. 6.

WAR DIARY
or
INTELLIGENCE SUMMARY.
(Erase heading not required.)

Place	Date	Hour	Summary of Events and Information	Remarks and references to Appendices
H.Q.	18/t Aug 1917		Ref Map 36° N.W. 1/20000	
G23h.3.3			On our own front situation has been very quiet during this period. Hostile aircraft has been very active and our M.G's with the help of tracer bullets has successfully kept them beyond their own lines. On the 21st Aug we drove a hostile aeroplane down in its aerodrome. I appeared to be slightly damaged by our M.G. bullets.	B.U.
	25/27 Aug 1917		Nothing unusual has happened in this front during this period, the situation has been very quiet except for occasional shelling on our Support and Reserve Lines and Communication Trenches. The enemy has devoted himself very freely principally round PUITS 13 and the outskirts of VENDIN. Much traffic of lorries and lames has been seen at VENDIN. Smoke can be seen rising from FOSSE 10 de LENS, built at night and early morning. Our M.Guns has continued harassing fire. road might on AULLUCH and the approaches to it & road bend at H.30.4.20.10, SUNKEN ROADS M.C. and COMMUNICATION trenches and TRENCH JUNCTIONS.	B.U.
	28-8-17 & 29-8-17		Ref 137 Inf. Brigade Order No. 162. In connection with these two raids we face the usual protection	27? 10F f—m? & ?pp?l.? 3 OR fm ?pl?l

A6945 Wt.W1422/M1160 35,000 12/16 D.D.&L. Forms/C/2118/14.

WAR DIARY
or
INTELLIGENCE SUMMARY.
(Erase heading not required.)

Army Form C. 2118.

137 M. Gun Company
No. 7.

Place	Date	Hour	Summary of Events and Information	Remarks and references to Appendices
H.Q.	28/7/17		Ref. Sheet 36c N.W. 1/20000.	28/7 1 O.R. to Hospital
G2 B 6.3.3	Aug 1917		Fine. The area raided was enemy's front & second line trenches from H.25.6.51.61 & H.19.d.32.12 and H.25.6.75.78 & H.19.a.56.15. This raid was carried out by 6 Officers and 160 O.Rs. of ½ S. Staffords Regt. at 8.3 p.m. The 2nd Raid was carried out by 6 Officers & 100 O.Rs. of 1 K.S. Staffs. Regt. The 2nd Raiding party in addition to above also raided enemy's 3rd line from H.25.t.80.20 & H.19.d.70.20. To assist the M.G. Barrage 24 guns were used as follows:- 10 guns of 137 M.G. Company, 8 guns of 178 M.G. Coy and 4 guns of 16 M.G. Coy the latter being situated on our RIGHT. These 4 guns fired on BOIS HUGO and it was thought probable that enemy caught fire naked M. G3 on our railway party from the wood. 2 guns of 178 M.G. Coy from H.24.c.45.30 swept road joining fire HONEY ALLEY and JUNCTION of HONEY and HURRELL trenches. Remainder of guns barraged round the area raided as follows. The ⅘th of HURREN TRENCH from HONEY ALLEY to H.19 c 9.7. HOBBS ALLEY. HIVE ALLEY HINDOO ALLEY HIGH TRENCH special attention being paid	

Army Form C. 2118.

WAR DIARY
or
INTELLIGENCE SUMMARY.
(Erase heading not required.)

137 M. Gun Coy.
No 8.

Place	Date	Hour	Summary of Events and Information	Remarks and references to Appendices
H.Q.	23/8/17		Ref. Sheet 36" N.W. 1/20000	
G.23.b.3.3	Aug 1917		to all TRENCH JUNCTIONS and in the area. The SUNKEN ROAD at H19d and H20c. Most of the barrages were done from RESERVE TRENCH at a range of about 2000 yds. Rates of fire, 1st Round Zero to minus & Zero + 6 for 10 rds per minute. From Zero to 6 'NUCLEAR'. 50 rds per minute 2nd Round. Zero+6 to Zero+8 100 rds per minute. Zero+8 to 'ALL CLEAR' 50 rds per minute. Over 12 guns operated above who, during these operations. The mule teams though successfully carried out in the hard road as captured 7 prisoners, & were billed before we could get them to our own lines. & 2 were wounded.	G.R.U.
	24/8/17		The 16th M. Gun Coy took over from us at Galloway position R.41 (G.24.d.29.72), BAY 17 (G.24.d.26.41) - the RESERVE LINE and POSEN ALLEY GUN (at H.25.a.38.85) in the SUPPORT line. Relief commenced at 6 p.m. and was finished at 7.30 p.m. The whole cow to this 1 Battery (of 4 guns) at H.Q. used for harassing fire and 1 Section in RESERVE at MARINCAR B.G.	B.R.U.

Army Form C. 2118.

WAR DIARY
or
INTELLIGENCE SUMMARY.
(Erase heading not required.)

137 M. Gun Coy
No. 9.

Place	Date	Hour	Summary of Events and Information	Remarks and references to Appendices
H.Q.	30/8/19	Ref Sheet 36° N.W. 1/40000	Weather very wet and dismal activity very little artillery activity 11k opposite	11k opposite 4K meridian
C.23.b.3.3			An enemy battalion was reported to be near approaching from GARVIN to MEVERGNIN at 11.30 a.m. this morning	BLU
	31-8-17		The front line in our left HALBERSTADTER musters where flights was not his own very short. East night until DAWN today we fired 6000 rds with 1 battery (4 guns) onto Tournal Enterance, LIGHT RAILWAY (H301) and TRENCH MORTAR Emplacement. In response to Canadian SOS signals on our RIGHT we fired 7000 rds with 3 guns onto our Canadian S.O.S. barrage line.	BLU
			Total Reinforcements for the month 4	Reinforcements for reinforcements 2
			Total Wounded 6	
			Sick to Hospit 10	
			From Hospit 5	
			Evacuated to C.C.S. 1	

E. R. Lawrence
O.C. 137 M. Gun Company

Army Form C. 2118.

137 M.G. Coy
No 1.
Vol 20

WAR DIARY
or
INTELLIGENCE SUMMARY.
(Erase heading not required.)

Place	Date	Hour	Summary of Events and Information	Remarks and references to Appendices
HQ G.23.c.33	1st Sept 1917	Ref 36c NW. 1/20000.	We fired 6000 rounds into HULLUCH and 3000 rounds in enfilade with Divi. Order No 227. Hostile aircraft was fairly active, six planes crossing our lines bet. 6am and 9am. These were fired on by our AA guns. A train was seen proceeding backwards and forwards between VENDIN and WINGLES; and a motor-lorry in the WINGLES — VENDIN Road. Two limbers and a small party of men were seen on the above road.	
	2nd Sept 1917		5000 rounds were fired on enemy light Railway. Hostile aircraft again active — 21 planes crossing our lines. Our AA guns fired 1300 rounds. Considerable enemy movements were observed in the area DOUVRIN — WINGLES and VENDIN — Horsemen & motor-cyclists being seen S.E. of WINGLES.	Lok M Hights
	3rd Sept 1917		5000 rounds were fired on enemy light Railway, Tunnel entrance and emplacements & on movement of Track (the last was visibly effective) Further aerial activity — eight planes crossing at great height — notified. Considerable movement was observed near PITS 13 and on road in H.15.	LM from Hights

WAR DIARY
or
INTELLIGENCE SUMMARY.
(Erase heading not required.)

137 Machine Gun Coy
No. 2

Place	Date	Hour	Summary of Events and Information	Remarks and references to Appendices
H.Q.	4th		Ref Sheet 36° N.W. 1/20,000	
			3500 rounds were fired on Track in H14d and on T.M. emplacement	1 O.R. wounded
G.23.b 3.3	5 Sept 1917		Two enemy planes flew over our lines at a great height towards NOEUX-LES-MINES yesterday	
			Enemy unusually partly observed at Trench in H16a+e. Movement was observed at PUITS 13 and between it and CITÉ ST LEONARD. Transport was heard during the night in CITÉ ST ELIE	
	5 Sept 1917		1 Battery fired 5000 rounds on track in H14d. Enemy opened heavy bombardment	1 O.R. killed
			at midnight on back areas which lasted for two hours	
			Considerable aerial activity during day - six planes attempted to cross our lines several times. They were eventually driven off by A.A. gun and M-gun fire. One of our planes was completely destroyed by enemy aeroplanes above the HOHENZOLLERN REDOUBT	
			Gas shells were fired into MAZINGARBE from 1 a.m. to 3 a.m.	
	6.7.17		1 Battery fired 4500 rds on LIGHT RWY in H.20.a + Tracks in H.14.c.	2 O.R. wounded
			Enemy aircraft very active, 2000 rds were expended on them in an attempt to drive them off	to C.C.S.
			Lorrance observed also MINE ALLEY in H.21.a	
			Situation normal.	

Army Form C. 2118.

WAR DIARY
or
INTELLIGENCE SUMMARY.
(Erase heading not required.)

137 Austrian Siege Bty.

Place	Date	Hour	Summary of Events and Information	Remarks and references to Appendices
			Ref Sheet. 36c N.W. 1/20,000	
	7.9.17		1 Battery fired on HULLUCH T main approaches trench 5500 rds.	
MAZINGARBE			Enemy Aircraft very quiet.	
	8.9.17		Ivanvelde observed a Tank at M.14.α.	
			We fired with 1 Battery on K. SCHOOLHOUSE T. Vicinity of CHURCH HULLUCH 3000 rds.	
			Enemy aircraft fairly active but at a great height, bombarded at 12 & 15 A.M. at him.	
			Our R.48 Photogs given at G.18.8. 94.18 that good results with bombing at small portions of the enemy in TRACK H M.H. during the day. Hit at 3 out of a party of 6.7 one at two others at [illegible] Chinese remounders they come to their knees & continued empting this area made the	
			enemy very angry & the Track is not used now frequently as before. We use got undertaken for return to the photos of S.19.3 & completes dulls, trench and drainage shown to portion	
	9.9.17		So consultation with a hint by the 137 F.Bty in our line 10.8 am trench fired on chequered target SOUTH of the Raiders. We fired at the rate of 150 rds per minute from 2 us to	
			2 en +7 & from 2 us +7 to 2 and +45 at 60 rds per minm. Total rounds fired 20,500	
			OUR RESERVE TRENCH was heavily shelled at 10 pm to 10.40 pm of them. 37 taken after the	
			raid. Zero hour for the Raid was 7.85 pm.	
			The Raid was carried out successfully. No casualties to the Raiders crossed the Enemy	
			line but tried to find any signs of the enemy, the enemy as having shelled to his support lines.	

WAR DIARY
or
INTELLIGENCE SUMMARY.
(Erase heading not required.)

137 Machine Gun Coy
No. 4

Army Form C. 2118.

Place	Date	Hour	Summary of Events and Information	Remarks and references to Appendices
MAZINGARBE	10.9.17		Ref. Sheet 36c N.W. 1/20,000	
			1 Battery fired to HULLUCH, Railway Redts & Cuir Rd at M.14.b. 2.1½. 4500 being expended.	
			Enemy aircraft fairly quiet. 2 Enemy hostile planes flying low at a great height over our lines.	
			Owing to cool starry night gun flashes movement by the enemy has been observed which the [illegible]	
			The RESERVE LINE has been sniped to one or two aerial Torpedos which made a crater of enormous size 15ft in depth & 25ft wide.	DH
	11.9.17		Our Battery fired on enemy Emplacements at M.13.b from dusk till dawn. 4000 rds	1 OR to Hospital
			Enemy aircraft inactive. The RESERVE LINE was sniped again & continued shelling by 4.2" & also Minenwerfer.	DH
	12.9.17		We fired with 1 Battery throughout the night again on Enemy Emplacements at M.13.b, M.13.10 & 25.15 3500 rds being expended.	1 OR to Hospital wounded R.K. C.C.S
			Three enemy planes crossed our lines between 6 & 7 pm & were fired on by our Guns 350 rds.	
			Continuation of shelling of our RESERVE LINE & also Minenwerfer close to our R+L Centre	DH

WAR DIARY
or
INTELLIGENCE SUMMARY.
(Erase heading not required.)

Army Form C. 2118.

137 Trench Mortar Bty No. 5

Place	Date	Hour	Summary of Events and Information	Remarks and references to Appendices
MAZINGARBE	13.9.17	Ref. Sheet 36c N.W. 1/20,000	Enemy fired salvos with his Artillery especially on our RESERVE LINE. Trench Mortars 13R & H. & H.yd. also active on R.4d position. 1 Battery fired 4500 rds on enemy Tunnel entrance at H.14.C.90.90. 10R. Harded & cemented. Enemy QUICK trug towards the close of the day between 6 & 7 pm.	B.T.
	14.9.17		Shelling of our RESERVE LINE with Whiz-bangs & also a few trenchmortars. Visibility bad & no sniping from R.49 posn. 1 Battery fired 5000 rds throughout the night on HULLUCH GUN EMPLACEMENT. Enemy QUICK & M.Gs.	B.T.
	15.9.17		Our 9th AVENUE BATTERY fired 5000 rds on TRACK H.14.a.7.1 & TRACK H.13.b.5.2. One of our snipers M.Gs. did good service at a group of the enemy on TRACK H.14.d. our men were seen to fall wounded. The Track quickly dispersed. Sniping shots were at many groups near H.7.C. during the day many of the enemy men seen to run & take cover.	B.T.

Army Form C. 2118.

137 Machine Gun Coy
No. 6

WAR DIARY
or
INTELLIGENCE SUMMARY.
(Erase heading not required.)

Instructions regarding War Diaries and Intelligence Summaries are contained in F. S. Regs., Part II. and the Staff Manual respectively. Title pages will be prepared in manuscript.

Place	Date	Hour	Summary of Events and Information	Remarks and references to Appendices
MAZINGARBE	16.9.17		Throughout the night an Battery fired 3000 rds on TRACKS at H.14a & H.14c.	
			We fired 2000 rds during the day at enemy aircraft which were fairly active between 5.30 p.m & 7.30 p.m. Little movement is observed in TRACK H.14 c. out and entrenched enfilade.	
			Enemy artillery fairly quiet.	N
	17.9.17		One of our Batteries harassed the common TRACKS H.14 c also TRENCHES entrance H.13 d. firing 5000 rds throughout the night.	
			Enemy aircraft active towards the close of day. We fired 1500 rds at enemy planes.	
			In vicinity of Port 13 is a nest at from during the day took with caution by the enemy. Little shelling during the day.	N
	18.9.17		3 balloons very quiet. 1 Battery fired 4000 rds on TRACKS & TRENCH in H.14 c & H.13 d. 10 h. Harrand	
				N
	19.9.17		1 Battery fired 4500 rds on selected Targets. H.14 6 1.2 & M.20 f 7.4. Alse. M.14 f 8.8 & M.20 a 1.2.	
			Enemy aircraft very active hunted the day our guns were firing at them & causing the planes to climb.	

Army Form C. 2118.

WAR DIARY
or
INTELLIGENCE SUMMARY.
(Erase heading not required.)

137 Machine Gun Coy.
No. 7

Place	Date	Hour	Summary of Events and Information	Remarks and references to Appendices
MAZINGARBE	19.9.17		Ref. Sheet 36c N.W. 1/20,000 Our Stokes M.G. fired 200 rds at different hrs on the enemy who away fr. remnants of H86 26.90 & round of K. having new aim fr. rounds down	A.
	20.9.17		On engagements with an armed each day by one of H. Batteries. The 52 N°2 section fired at perished Guns fired 5000 rds on Targets H70d 10.35 & H13& 95.70. Enemy aircraft very quiet during the day. Our L.G. Guns caught at several of the enemy any Trench at H146 & succeeded in wounding sev. men. Signal wire observed on both sides of enemy's trench at VENDIN LIEVIN.	A.
	21.9.17		1 Battery fired 5000 rds on Trench H13& 96. During the day we fired 750 rds on enemy aircraft. Returned very quick on our front & Little artillery activity.	B.
	22.9.17		One Battery fired 4,500 rds to enemy's Communication Trenches in H.7c & Road to H.108. Considerable aerial activity for which day 7 guns expending 2500 rds on enemy aircraft. Slight activity of our RESERVE LINE.	H.

Army Form C. 2118.

137 Machine Gun Coy
No. 8

WAR DIARY
OF
INTELLIGENCE SUMMARY.
(Erase heading not required.)

Instructions regarding War Diaries and Intelligence Summaries are contained in F. S. Regs., Part II. and the Staff Manual respectively. Title pages will be prepared in manuscript.

Place	Date	Hour	Summary of Events and Information	Remarks and references to Appendices
MAZINGARBE	23.9.17		Ref. Sheet. 36c NW 1/20,000 Our indirect fire Battery moved to CURZON ST. at G.25.d 99.70.	
			Enemy aircraft very quiet. Slight activity on Front at H.14 60.15	M
			Intense bombardment near HILL 70 at 10 p.m.	
	24.9.17		1. Battery fired 4000 rds into E. Trench + Tracks adjoining BOIS HUGO + BOIS QUATORZE in H.26 & H.27 + also VENDIN RD. to H.20 d.	
			Enemy communication on our right on HILL 70. Heavy bombardment at 5 p.m. also on our Back area	
			The bombardment seemed to be miscellaneous between BOIS MAROC + CITÉ ST PIERRE + behind M.	
			2/2 Lieu. Lowry Rockes. Enemy aircraft very active + 14 planes being seen at one time.	
			Movement near front in Aid Section (very intricate)	M
	2.59.17		Throughout the night we harassed the enemy in HULLUCH by firing 3000 rds into the Valley 126.5.14dd	
			Aerial activity of the enemy slight during the morning.	
			Enemy M.G. also firing from H.13a 20.70 at 8 hr.	
			Enemy artillery been shelling at BULL.	
			Enemy MG located at H.13a 32.43. Sixty observed today over the project.	M

A6945 Wt. W11422/M1160 35,000 12/16 D.D.&L. Forms/C./2118/14.

WAR DIARY or INTELLIGENCE SUMMARY

Army Form C. 2118.

137 Brigade Infantry No. 9

Place	Date	Hour	Summary of Events and Information	Remarks and references to Appendices
MAZINGARBE	26.4.17	Rel. Stat. 36 c.N.N. 1/40,000	1 Battery fired two bursts of fire down on HEMLOCK ALLEY & Trenches N. of HULLUCH. 3000 rds. Enemy sniping very active throughout the day. T alias N.C. 10 S.O.S. an enemy flare was exploded & two enemy front line posts N.132.c.8.0. by long distance lights. Fire of two enemy wiring parties observed & burst in M.I.R. Heavy fire on our front on our Suffolk front. Enemy seen engaged throwing from M.132. 20.70. during the night, came front firing in HIN ALLEY & RESERVE TRENCH.	10 k. killed 4 k wounded
	27.4.17		1 Battery fired sustained fire at night on FOSSE 8 TRENCHES in HULLUCH. 3000 rds. Enemy sniping tried to harass in the early morning but rather very quiet. Gas at CITE ST ELIE Lamp trickrock against light was observed at 11.30pm. Gun was projected over an ord N/E N.C. 1am in Trench Junction Corner. Enemy M.G.S were very active, sweeping on RESERVE TRENCH through R.4.K & K.4 front firing for night.	1 N.R. wounded 4 k. wounded

WAR DIARY or INTELLIGENCE SUMMARY

Army Form C. 2118.

137 Machine Gun Coy
No. 10

Place	Date	Hour	Summary of Events and Information	Remarks and references to Appendices
MAZINGARBE	28.9.17		Ref 36cNW 1/20,000. Enemy aircraft quite normal. Seven enemy aircraft followed one of this morning from dawn to everlasting Hill 70.	1DEC.H/1/4
			Our RESERVE TRENCH was shelled at 3pm between Reg Points T NINGS NAY by 4.2's	
			Enemy M.G. turned fire from H.13a 20.70.	
			Our Battery fired 3500 rds on HULLUCH MAIN RD at H.14a 35.70.	
	29.9.17		Enemy aircraft very active. At 5.55am the enemy planes flying high over our lines met an three E.A. which crashed down into hostile landing crown down suddenly & attacked one of enemy airmen landing	
			in front of NINGLES WATER TOWER. Another E.A. attacked on ground & apparently demolished at 1 Officer Airfield.	
			& fired his gun away followed by the E.A. When the E.A. got very close to our position, our A.A.M.G. at R.48 Central & chased the truck at a range of about 500 ft at the E.A. doing excellent shooting. The E.A. immediately swerved & turned away flying back to the lines. It was impossible for our planes were able to return back again into our lines.	
			The Infantry retired towards it. The E.A. was seen to nosedive in front of NINGLES.	
			Our indirect Battery fired 3500 rds on FOSSE & TRACKS in H.14Cd.	

WAR DIARY
or
INTELLIGENCE SUMMARY.
(Erase heading not required.)

Army Form C. 2118.

137 Machine Gun Coy
No. 11

Place	Date	Hour	Summary of Events and Information	Remarks and references to Appendices
MAZINGARBE	30.9.17		Ref Sheet 36c N.W. 1/20,000	18k R. Hopkirk
			A.A. Battery fired at Enemy Machine Gun Emplacements & Trenches at M.20.c. 2000 rds.	
			Coys A.A. Guns at K.4.B. T.K.4.B fired during the day 2000rds at E.A.	
			Enemy Aircraft very quiet.	
			Heavy enemy Trench Mortar shoot on MULYCH at 10.30 pm. Knocked entirely of Trenches & men.	
			Total Reinforcements to 6 Sections. 1 (sens)	
			7. L. L. Wounded. 2	
			Sick & Hospital 5	
			Flesh Hopkirk 2	
			Evacuated to C.C.S. 4	
			Reported sick Evacuated 3	
			Sworn Harry Lieut.	
			O.C. 137 Machine Gun Coy	

WAR DIARY or INTELLIGENCE SUMMARY

Army Form C. 2118.

137th Machine Gun Coy.

October 1917

No. 1

Place	Date	Hour	Summary of Events and Information	Remarks and references to Appendices
MAZINGARBE	1.10.17		1 Battery shot harassing fire during the night on HULLUCH MAIN ROADS & TRACKS, WOODS. Ref Sheet 36c N.W. 1/20,000	Vol 21
			Enemy aircraft very active. 8 Albatros Scouts were driven off by our A.A. Guns when they attempted to cross the lines. M.G.'s not fired on an enemy plane which dive bombed & turned to the	
			Direct wire MINGLES & VENDIN	
			Enemy artillery quiet but H.T.M. active	
2.10.17		In comparison with an organised bombardment of battery lines on enemy Barrack & main Communications in front 10,000 rds. We fired 6 guns & discharged from G.S.d. 23.62 G.S.d. 12.85 & G.S.d. 36 & G.S.d. 22.75. Our guns shot bursts on the camel heights & known as	
			the Ridges. Enemy aircraft fairly about at times but did not observe any Albatros Scouts attached on J.m.	
			we observed bursts with & accuracy. We opened to enemy from front on A.A. guns.	
			Two enemy planes on M.G.'s were fired at & a great height coming up by our M.G's.	
			Our Shell were fired on our back area by the enemy at 10 p.m.	

October 1917.

WAR DIARY
INTELLIGENCE SUMMARY.
(Erase heading not required.)

137th Trench Mortar Bty.
Army Form C. 2118.
No. 2

Place	Date	Hour	Summary of Events and Information	Remarks and references to Appendices
MAZINGARBE	3.10.17	Ref Sheet 36cNW 1/20,000	1 Battery fired 2500 rds on Enemy Trench Entrance & Trench Junction Emplacement & on Rd LIGHT RWY at M.20.a throughout the night. Enemy retaliation about over Hill 70 but very slight. Artillery very quiet.	2.T.O.B. Reinforcements
	4.10.17		MG fired on HOLLUCH & man Alleys about onto HULLUCH TRENCH. Rounds fired 2,500. Retaliation slight during the day owing to low visibility. Situation very quiet.	TOR 1st Lt... 1 Other.. Transferred to 105 Bn. [signature]
	5.10.17		About 7.30 pm much trench was seen & heard on HILL 70 followed by Trench Mortars & slight enemy Artillery bombardment, the enemy attempted a raid but were repulsed. In response to our S.O.S. call our M.G's fired 20,000 on their S.O.S. Targets. This small raid lasted until about 9.30 pm when all was quiet again. At 11.40 pm an Archangel Gun on the W of our front during this operation fire Bay 17 tally 1, CURZON ST, R45A to fired in allotted Targets, the rate of firing from 2rds +½ to 2rds + 10 125 rds per minute from time until the Artillery stopped 60 per min. 12,500 being fired. Enemy artillery action in the morning, our gunner succeeded in driving off 2 enemy scouts.	1.O.B. to Hospital

October 1917

WAR DIARY
INTELLIGENCE SUMMARY.
(Erase heading not required.)

Army Form C. 2118.

137 Howitzer Bm Bty
1/3

Place	Date	Hour	Summary of Events and Information	Remarks and references to Appendices
MAZINGARBE	5.10.17		Ref. Sheet. 36c N.W. 1/20,000. Bty fired on enemy park, the enemy park, the enemy MG's are very active. Enemy sniping on RESERVE LINE. Fuse 106 been sent up.	
	6.10.17		In conjunction with a raid by the 137th Bde on our left. Bty fired from 2 us + 1/2 to 2 us + 10 & 125 rds per minute. Then hove burst artillery channel 60 rds per minute. R. 46 fired on Target G.8.6 3.6 & G.8.b. 22.75 & R.41 on Target G.8.c 23.62 & G.8.d 12.28. Total number of rounds fired 4,500.	
			1 Battery fired on enemy MT Dump at H.21.a 45.60 & R. CURZON St BATTERY fires & harassed HERCULES TRENCH at H.20.6. Rounds fired 350. Enemy aeroplane active between 7.30am & 9.30am. Our R.4.5 guns carried out small shoots of enemy strong points near M.14.c 30.15. & firing action to the guns on small shoots at M.14.c 9.6. Tonight Bde fired Parts 13 & 4 of shoot, starting, Irish ditches 4.0. & 4.30 am	
	7.10.17		1 Battery fired 100 rds into HULLUCH + on the HULLUCH MAIN R.D. Enemy artillery was retaliated very but activity of weather.	

October 1917.

WAR DIARY
of
INTELLIGENCE SUMMARY.
(Erase heading not required.)

Army Form C. 2118.

137 Infantry Brigade Coy
4

Place	Date	Hour	Summary of Events and Information	Remarks and references to Appendices
MAZINGARBE	8.10.17		R/ Sheet 36c N.W. 1/20,000	
			During the early part of weather observation difficult	
			Enemy aircraft inactive	
			1 Battery fired 3500 rds on DUMP at H.13.d.00.55. T on HULLUCH MAIN ROAD from dusk till dawn	
			A small body of 4 men was seen on track behind HERCULES TRENCH in H.21.c. Gun's fired at	
			VENDIN.	DH
	9.10.17		1 Battery fired 1500 rds on DUMP at H.21.a & R.25 gun fired 1500 rds on TRACK in H.21.c	
			Aerial activity and enemy to that weather.	
			Increased rain in back area. RWY TRAIN between MAISNES & DOUVRIN on the PONT-A-VENDIN RWY at	
			B.25.b.	DH
			Enemy artillery active between 2pm & 5pm on G.22.6. Track	
	10.10.17		1 Battery fired 3000 rds on HULLUCH MAIN Rd + TRACK in H.21.c	
			Enemy transport active at 8.30am on A.A. gun's fired 2500 rds & was observed in back of train	10KL
			moving fire on him	Appl'd
			Transport train on HULLUCH between 7pm & 8pm	
				DH

October 1917.

WAR DIARY
INTELLIGENCE SUMMARY.

of A. Anderson from Log 137

Army Form C. 2118.

(Erase heading not required.)

Place	Date	Hour	Summary of Events and Information	Remarks and references to Appendices
MAZINGARBE B.5	11.10.17	Rel Shoe 36 & N.M. 4/20,000	In cooperation with an Artillery Emergency Embarkment & Battery fired on TRACK & COMMUNICATIONS	2.O.R. Col
			No men to the vicinity of the Artillery Target on as tough wanted Jallins. One gun fired 3000 to	5 Hospital
			and telle for open Enemy fired at the men seen in the Artillery observed at	
			Bat 6 Gun fired 1500 rds on HAMLET TRENCH & TRACK in H7R & H13t.	1.O.R. wounded to C.C.S. No 1
			Enemy artillery retaliated fruitlessly and at times MG's were very active.	
			During the morning we observed a flare of enemy working on top of their trenches owing to the bad	
			weather, which HELLVCH TRENCH	
	12.10.17		1 Battery fired on HEMLOCK ALLEY & TRACKS in H14c. 3000 rds. Enemy fired throughout the night	1.0.R. to Hospital
			Salvation every quiet owing to very bad weather conditions & in the observation	
	13.10.17		In cooperation with a divided Artillery Summary Embarkment which was carried out promptly on the Wm	
			on Bat 17 Battery again fired on TRACKS & COMMUNICATIONS, 2500 rds were fired.	
			Bat 6 Gun engaged M.G. & T.M. Emplacement in H7d. 380 rds were expended.	
			Enemy aircraft ack very active, an E.A. flew Left towards MAZINGARBE on A.A. gun firing & ack of	
			Range.	

October 1917

WAR DIARY or INTELLIGENCE SUMMARY

Army Form C. 2118.

137 Siege Battery R.G.A.
No. 16

Place	Date	Hour	Summary of Events and Information	Remarks and references to Appendices
MAZINGARBE	13/10/17		Ry/ Stat. 36.c N.W. 1/20,000. A good deal of movement was observed in the morning at H.27.a 60.10 between 6 am & 8 am about 150-200 of the enemy within a distance of 500 yds.	
			At 10 am a Train was observed behind MINGLES. The Heavy Artillery engaged this Target & a large explosion was observed near the RWY STATION. Artillery fairly quiet.	SM
	14/10/17		I Battery harassed HULLUCH throughout the night. 300 rds. Eng fired. Our A.A. guns fired 400 rds during the day. The enemy aircraft activity was very active throughout our guns succeeded several times in driving the enemy away; no enemy on any front. We a Taube flying in the air of the Allahines Sector before. Signalling was observed by our O.P. on Tower from EAST end of P.P. in H.15 & 1 towards VENAIN	1 S.S. with E Hospital.
			CHURCH at 2 pm for about 20 minutes. Artillery very quiet.	SM
	15/10/17		In conjunction with a attack made by the 1/5 Welsh. Staff Regt. an MG Battery at CURSON ST. front 3000 rds in mintures from 9.30 pm to 11 pm. Our fire was confirmed by the Raiders & caused bitter. At just 7.30 at Enemy aircraft flew from 10 am - 2.20 pm. Enemy artillery shelled chiefly of the road.	1 OR E Robert rescued to CCS N.Y. SM

October 1917.

WAR DIARY
INTELLIGENCE SUMMARY.
(Erase heading not required.)

137 Machine Gun Coy
No. 7

Army Form C. 2118.

Place	Date	Hour	Summary of Events and Information	Remarks and references to Appendices
MAZINGARBE	16.10.17		R/ Shot 36c N.W. 72.0,070. 1 Battery but down 2k on DUMP in H13.b. co.55 T TRACK in H.21.C. Investigated - No mgk. Enemy aircraft very active. 21 planes being seen during the day. On A.A. guns reaching an aerial observer in "taking" the enemy away from straying over our lines. 2000 rds own. Fired at enemy kite on A.A. guns. Artillery active at 12 noon on the RESERVE LINE. Signally "downed" in VENDIN at 6.15pm. This was being done by a given height.	1.O.K. wounded 4 S.S.Q. No.15. 1 O.R. to Hospital. No 20 found.
	17.10.17		1 Battery went over 2hs on HIVE ALLEY TRENCH & traversed in H.21A Investigated. No mgk. Ten E.A. planes seen during the day at various times. Own guns fired 1500 rds at this planes. & caused some to be bought down in our lines. Enemy artillery shelled our RESERVE LINE SOUTH of VENDIN ALLEY chiefly with 4.2.	1 O.K. wounded in action.
	18.10.17		Investigated no mgk at first & traversed & enemy on all his known shell holes & tracks in H.13.b & H.14.a. TRACK along HEMLOCK ALLEY in H14.a.7, HIVE ALLEY in H20.b & c, also HERCULES TRENCH and Transport. 13,000 rds own fired. R.47 gun opened at small bodies of the enemy in T's & shell holes on every TRACK in H13c 30.25.	

WAR DIARY / INTELLIGENCE SUMMARY

October 1917

137 Infantry Bde. Hqrs.
No. 8
Army Form C. 2118.

Place	Date	Hour	Summary of Events and Information	Remarks and references to Appendices
MAZINGARBE	18.10.17	Rel. Strath 36th N.H. H.Q. 12q.a.a.b	The enemy considerably checked & sent sun along the TRACK & roads to the French	
			The enemy aircraft were active but silent except at 4pm when 6 planes flew over our lines at about 2000 ft. & succeeded in keeping them high.	
			Several of the enemy were seen getting out of TRench in H20c 30.70 at 5.30 pm	
	19.10.17		Throughout the night 500 rds. were fired on TRACKS in H13d & H20b, VENDIN R⁴ & TRACK in H21c by our Battery at CURSON ST & BAY 17.	10 k. wounded
			E.A. active about dawn & 7 pm. on A.A. gun fired 1500 rds.	
			Small parties of the enemy in twos & fives were observed from an R47 position on TRACK in H21a 3.5.	1 O.R. wounded & killed
			2 Buy. attempted to be carried out aerial	
			Enemy Artillery active on our front line in H.Hill 70.	
	20.10.17		1 Battery fired occasional fire on the TRACK S. of BOIS DES DAMES between H20d 50.90 & H21a 50.70 200 ds. were fired. Everything quiet except alvin, I.E.A. being brought down right behind our lines at 1.30 pm (burnt). A total of 1200 rds. were expended on E.A.	1 gun sent to hospital
			Personnel relief done. HERCULES TRENCH H15c 20.50 small patrol carrying activities.	

October 1917.

WAR DIARY
INTELLIGENCE SUMMARY.
(Erase heading not required.)

Army Form C. 2118.

137 Pounder Siege Bty
No. 9

Place	Date	Hour	Summary of Events and Information	Remarks and references to Appendices
MAZINGARBE	21.10.17	Ref. Sheet 36c N.W. 1/20,000	Three of our guns 2 at CURSON ST. Battery + 1 at BAY 17 Battery fired on Jctn in the enemy wire at H.28.c.40.40 + H.28.c.30.70 + H.25.b.40.95. H.25.b. 6.25 gds wire fired until the break element in the morning. Three gaps cut twenty high. Clear for Infantry Raid.	I.O.K. [signatures] No 2.0.S.
			R.48 fired on the HULLUCH MAIN R.B. Trenching. Fire harassing the enemy. 1500 rds fired.	
			Artillery activity on the LENS front at 7.30 pm. Our Reserve line shelled by Med+ large	
			at 2.45 pm. Aerial activity nil.	[sig]
	22.10.17		Gaps in enemies wire still kept open at H.25.b + 60.40 H.28.b.30.70 + H.19.d.40.06. 1.O.K. unchanged	[signatures]
			The guns firing under daylight. 2500 rds were fired.	
			BAY 17 Battery fired on DUMP + HULLUCH TRENCH + H.20.d. 1500 rds.	
			1 E.A. (AVIATIK) flew over from MINGLES towards BOIS HUGO at 5 pm.	
			Enemy heavy bombarded BOIS HUGO at 5 pm.	[sig]
	23.10.17		Three of our guns at CURSON ST. fired 3500 rds on gap in enemy wire at H.25.b 50.90 + H.25.d 90.10 until dawn. BAY 17 Battery 1 gun fired in Sft at M.19.a.	

A6945 Wt. W14427/M1160 35,000 12/16 D.D. & L. Forms/C/2118/14.

WAR DIARY
INTELLIGENCE SUMMARY
(Erase heading not required.)

October 1917.

137 Machine Gun Coy
No. 10.

Army Form C. 2118.

Place	Date	Hour	Summary of Events and Information	Remarks and references to Appendices
MAZINGARBE	23/10/17		Ref. Sheet 36cN.W. 1/20,000	
			Enemy aircraft very active towards dusk. 5 Albatros Scouts fired on ours & anti A.A. fuel on by our A.A. guns. 1500 rds during enfilade fire returned towards WINGLES.	
			At 4.45pm 1 E.A. flew very low & fired about 100 rds into our RESERVE TRENCH & BROADWAY. R.4.3 fired 50 rds & the enemy plane returned quickly towards WINGLES.	S.H
			Enemy artillery quiet.	
	24/10/17		1 Battery fired 3000 rds throughout the night & 8pk open fire gaps in enemy wire at H.19.a.40.06.	" "
			" H.28.6.40.92.	
			1500 rds own fired on enemy DUMP at junction of HIVE ALLEY & HERCULES TRENCH.	
			Enemy aircraft slightly active towards dusk. 2 planes flying fired low altitude and lights fired & own and on an E. direction.	
			Enemy movement considerable in back areas. Parties of 50 & 60 along but by an open track. Many gun-limbs seen moving towards him from WINGLES. They carried HIVE ALLEY back H.2.14.20.20.	
			At 10.30 am Transport seen on frontage along track seen tied moving at H.30.70.30.	
			Slight artillery towards enemy.	S.H

WAR DIARY of INTELLIGENCE SUMMARY.

October 1917.

137th Kashmir Gun Coy No. 11

Army Form C. 2118.

Place	Date	Hour	Summary of Events and Information	Remarks and references to Appendices
MAZINGARBE	25/10/17		Ref Sheet 36c N.W. 1/20,000.	
			1 Ratling at CURZON ST. fired 6000 rds on enemy with gun at M25B 50 90. H25B 90.20 & H19d 40.06.	
			1500 rds were fired harassing enemy DUMP in HULLUCH at M13d 90 60. Enemy aircraft active owing to bad weather.	
			2. Enemy M.C. active South over CURZON ST. Ratting firing from a Mobile aircraft.	
			Slight activity of our own in GOHL Strongholds on Bay 17 Ratting at 7.30pm for 1/2 hour.	
			Bois des JAMES.	DJ
	26.10.17		CURZON ST. Ratling fired 4,500 on goth on enemy's wire from about the dawn.	
			An enemy M.C. which was sweeping the parapet of RESERVE TRENCH was silenced by the Ratling at 1.02 from Hostile.	
			Bay 17 Ratling to be firing from about H20c 40.65 HULLUCH TRENCH. One gun at BAY 17 had in it stuck + fired 1500 rds rapid at 7.45pm. The enemy gun did not fire again.	
			E.Aircraft active in the morning & 1 Enemy plane flying very low from MINGLES. Once we saw first two E.A. during the day.	
			8 Enemy Balloons up in the South in the morning.	DJ

October 1917

Army Form C. 2118.

WAR DIARY
INTELLIGENCE SUMMARY

137 Machine Gun Coy

No. 12

(Erase heading not required.)

Place	Date	Hour	Summary of Events and Information	Remarks and references to Appendices
MAZINGARBE	27.10.17		Ref Sheet. 36c N.W. 1/20,000 1/ Battery fired attack on "gap" in enemy wire at M25b 90.10, H25b 50.90, H19a 40.06, H25b 60.50, + H25b 84.20 from immediately dusk until dawn. BAY 17 Battery fired harassing fire throughout the night on the MULLOCH MAIN RD. 1500 rds. On enemy supposed trench of the enemy wire about H19a 20.20 also H19a 30.30. Enemy aircraft gave an alarm at 7.45 am from direction of BOIS DE DIX HUIT, (6 alterations) Flares. Enemy seen using these lights to direct fire of their A.A. guns on our planes at 10 pm.	I.O.R.K. wounded R No. 13 C.C.S. I.O.R. K. Case sent U.K. 10 O.R. Back (wounded)
	28.10.17		1st night an CURZON ST Battery fired 300 rds on bund on the gaps in the enemy wire at M25b 90.10, H25b 50.91, H19a 40.06 + H25b 84.20. BAY 17 Battery fired harassing fire on DUMP + HA. at H21a 45.60 throughout the night. 1500 rds. From 9 am to 10.30 am E.A. very active 7 planes from direction of BOIS DIX HUIT came over our line. One was quite high, they returned at 11 am. 4 more have flew on E.A. movement was seen around BOIS de QUATORZE in the morning. A land was head flying in BENEFONTAINE at 3 pm. The GOOSE (Minenwerfer) was firing yesterday but was silenced by our Artillery. Enemy shelled Junction of VENDIN ALLEY + RESERVE LINE throughout the morning with 77 mm. An American Officer was attached to this Coy for 3days to gain some practical experience.	1 Officer attached from Hospital Category B1

WAR DIARY
or
INTELLIGENCE SUMMARY
(Erase heading not required.)

Army Form C. 2118.

137 Infantry Bde HQ
No. 13

October 1917.

Place	Date	Hour	Summary of Events and Information	Remarks and references to Appendices
MAZINGARBE	29.10.17		Ref Sheet. 36 c N.W. 1/20,000. Ref Shk. 36 c N.W. Quiet night on CURSON ST. Battery fired 350 rds on gap in enemy wire as in Tr 28.5. per diem until visibility clear. Aircraft not very active, except 4 in the direction of HULLUCH, which were very high abt 9.30 p.m. As flt were observed in HULLUCH at 9h caused by our Aeroplane Bombs. Enemy trench Patrols observed going from South HULLUCH onward. In readiness for the "Broomstick Raid" on Tr 38 front, one gun filed as arranged on gap in enemy wire. 300 rds on enemy field.	
	30.10.17		Ref. 1st Battery harassed the tramways M.A. & DUMP at HZ1A 45.60. Harassed Tr. night. Enemy aircraft very active, 1 E.A. shot down on our front lines at 10.30 am & our pilot on parachute. All shipping of enemy clear from our new 1550 front being filed. One of our planes was brought down at 10.40 am behind HULLUCH by the enemy A/A.	L.O.R.
	31.10.17		At 4.32 pm a demonstration raid was carried out on the enemy front & support trenches in H15c & by the 4th Lanc Staff Riffs. remaining in the enemy trench & port 40 minutes. The object of the raid was to kill as many of the enemy as possible & to secure identification. The raiders assembled on Tr trench line Red HULLUCH BOYAUX S6 + 62. The raid was preceded by a dummy attack opposite HULLUCH which consisted of a drifting of dummy figures South BOYAUX & rifle bombardment. This was an attempt on following the support front of the...	

October 1917

WAR DIARY
INTELLIGENCE SUMMARY
(Erase heading not required.)

Army Form C. 2118.

137 Machine Gun Coy.
No. 14

Place	Date	Hour	Summary of Events and Information	Remarks and references to Appendices
MAZINGARBE	3/10/17	N.M. 12.00 a.m	The Machine Guns of this company assisted other in the O Sunday Raid @ The Raid.	

① 1 gun at (R48) G.24.b covering HERRING ALLEY from H.13.d 15.44 to H.13.d 32.54
  1 gun at (R48) G.18.a enfilading HULLUCH TRENCH from H.13.d 52.03 to H.19 & 74.92

② The R. RAID :—
  R.46 at G.19.d } to enfilade trench running from H.26.a 15.73 to H.26.a 36.82
  R.47 at G.19.c }
  B.H.V. Battery of 2 guns at G.24.b sweeping HULLUCH Trench from H.20.c 65.15 to H.26.a 94.83
  CURSON ST Battery of 3 guns at G.24.d sweeping Trench from MK.t 65.95 to front trench H.26.a 15.74
  CURSON ST " of 1 gun at G.24.d engaged hostile M.G. fire at H.19.c 99.62
  R.47 at G.18.d enfilaced trench & neutralized M.G. at H.20.c 30.90

  Zero hour was 4.32 p.m. all guns fired from 2 secs + ½ to 2 secs + 5 minutes. Rapid fire 2 secs + 5 to all clear. Works for wounded. Barrage R.48 guns which fired rapid fire from 2 secs. to 2 minutes was a belt of 80,000 rds was fired during the Raid.
  The whole Raid was entirely successful, the infantry killing a many of the enemy, returning in 10 days with full & capturing 48 Prisoners of the 10 R.I.R. 213 R.I.R. & 9 J. Division. Our own casualties in the M.G. Sup. Btn. were under 10, and very slight. None wounded of the Russians including a Corporal posted on Machine Gun fire was very slight & infantile none casualties

October 1917

137 Southern Div Coy
No. 15

Army Form C. 2118.

WAR DIARY
or
INTELLIGENCE SUMMARY.
(Erase heading not required.)

Place	Date	Hour	Summary of Events and Information	Remarks and references to Appendices
MAZINGARBE	31/10/17	Ref Sk.C. See N.W. Pen. org	Our artillery cooperated during the Raid by the cutting of the enemy's wire entanglements on HULLUCH to H.14.a. subtile SLAG HEAP H.14.c. 30.18. I engaged MG for the enemy trenches. The enemy offered little or no opposition on all the wires the Raid.	
			Total Reinforcements for the month ... 6	
			Total Wounded ... 2	
			Sick to Hospital ... 7 (1 officer)	
			From Hospital ... 3 (1 officer)	
			Evacuated to C.C.S. ... 6	
			Rejoined after Evacuation ... 1	
			Transferred to 125 Division ... 1 (officer)	
			To Cadre School U.K. ... 1	
			To Base invalid ... 1	

Norman Harvey, Lt.
f.O.C. 137 M.G.Coy

To H.Q.
137 Bde.

> No. 137
> MACHINE GUN
> COMPANY.
> No.
> Date 2.12.17

Herewith War Diary of 137th M.G. Coy. for the month of November 1917.

Leslie R. G. Heriot Lt.
for Capt.
Commanding
137 M.G. Coy.

WAR DIARY / INTELLIGENCE SUMMARY

137 Machine Gun Coy
Army Form C. 2118.
No. 1/M 22

Place	Date	Hour	Summary of Events and Information	Remarks and references to Appendices
MAZINGARBE	1.11.17		A/Sht 36cNW. 1/20,000. In cooperation with artillery shoots carried out from 5.40 pm to 12.17 am on selected targets, our Machine Guns working in cooperation, fired 9800 rounds, in the vicinity of the Artillery targets, as far as our range would allow. We also did some harassing fire on HULLUCH MAIN RD. & SCHOOL HOUSE from which 2000 rounds were fired. There was no aerial activity owing to dull weather. Enemy Machine Guns were a little more active firing from C.K. St. ELIE, a building crossing our Artillery retaliation was very slight during our Gunnery operations.	
	2.11.17		On night of 1st to 2nd he fired 1500 rounds from Curzon St on the enemy railway at HA21a H0=55, also 2 guns at R45 into PUITS13, a further 3500 rounds were fired at PUITS 13, from BAY 17 Railway dump & RKS. There was no aerial activity.	1 O.R. wounded

WAR DIARY
INTELLIGENCE SUMMARY
(Erase heading not required.)

Army Form C. 2118.

137½ M.G. Coy.
No. 2.

Place	Date	Hour	Summary of Events and Information	Remarks and references to Appendices
MAZINGARBE	3.11.17		Ref Sheet 36 c. N.W. 1/2,000 We fired from our CURSON N S.E. Battery 500 rounds on the HULLUCH TRENCH in H 13 b & 4250 rounds on enemy front line between HOBBS & HONEY ALLEY, also 1500 rounds fired into PEIRIS 13, between 6 p.m. & 12 mid-night, in addition to this a further 1500 rounds on Dump & Tramway at H21a+0.51- at 10.46 am the following day, enemy working parties were observed walking about near junction of HOBBS ALLEY & HULLUCH trench. In addition, fired 100 rounds at them, from one of our Right Section guns, forty were disposed.	1 O.R. Y58ac.support (Untraced)
	4.11.17		In conjunction with the raid by the 139th Lt. Bde. teams of our guns of Bay 17 & one of R's fired 5000 rounds on the following targets. One gun to enfilade enemy front line from H 26 c 78.67 to A 26 d 05.50, one gun to enfilade enemy front line at H 26 d 15.35 & the 3rd gun to enfilade enemy front from H 26 c 58.75 to H 26 c 74.65. The order for this operation was issued by Order 258. The barrage to our artillery for the raid was not answered by the enemy guns until 5.13 a.m. at Hill 70 was shelled along the railway 6.140 p.m. the enemy then traversed with whizz-bangs along to the RESERVE trench, about 20 shells landing round our R's Pan & 15 close to our Battery at 15 A 1, 2, 4. In accordance with Orders, our guns were also ready for the 138 & 24. Art. raid, but this being cancelled, our guns were at once switched on to their S.O.S. Targets lines, which enemy kept up an intermittent bombardment until 10 p.m after which the usual quiet was resumed. Hostility was not during the day.	1 O.R. to hospital (sick)

WAR DIARY / INTELLIGENCE SUMMARY

137th Ar. Bde. No. 3.

Place	Date	Hour	Summary of Events and Information	Remarks and references to Appendices
MAZINGARBE	5.11.17		Ref Sheet 36.c N.W. 1/20,000 In accordance with instructions from Divisional order 259 for the 138 I.F. Bde. raid, our guns at R.46-R.47-R.45a & b HAY ALLEY NORTH, were laid on their respective targets, & the one, "called upon" by "Signal", this signal was sent to fire only. 30 bm. fire went over at once switched on to this sent, 30 bm. fire grds & from dusk onwards our Battery at Coram St. S.O.S. night lines. On firing of Aindoc ALLEY & Hulluch # trench. fired 2500 rounds on firing of Aindoc ALLEY & Hulluch # trench. Gas was sent over by the R.F. How. emplacement was sent up a double R.48 position. At 10.5 p.m. in reply to enemy sent up a double green & turtle Red light in behind the Craters, 20 minutes later 2 Salvoes from night guns were pinned on to area between HAY ALLEY & N. WINGS WAY. There is now a large Red Cross flag flying in a trench near track in Huad. This track, our gun at R.48 has worried continually with the assistance of the O.T. at BUNRATTY. parties of the enemy often being observed along track & at once sniped at. Some have been seen hit & killed or severely wounded. JT	I.O.R. from Hospital

WAR DIARY

INTELLIGENCE SUMMARY

(Erase heading not required.)

Army Form C. 2118.

137th M.G. Coy.
7.O. 4.D.

Place	Date	Hour	Summary of Events and Information	Remarks and references to Appendices
MAZINGARBE	6.11.17	Ref. Sheet 36 C 1/20,000, N.W.	In accordance with information received from 137 A.T. + B.T. were c/o 1/350. Two Guns at CURZON ST. fired on tracks at H.29.c.v.d. in conjunction with harassing fire by artillery, rounds fired were 2000, at A.45. Position. Two fired 400 rounds at Guns, 12 outbursts 1 air. R.47 + R.48 Guns also fired 1500 rounds on Targets A.1 & B.5.1.20 + H.7.8.9.5.7.30. In addition to this our Battery of B.4.17.7th fired at an enemy trench mortar battery in H.15.a.05.63, firing burst 6 between. A plane was overhead, about interests between 7p.m. + 12 midnight.	1. O.R. returned 4/65. } succession
	7.11.17		Our guns at CURZON ST. Battery fired 5000 rounds on DUMP & HULLUCH in H.13.6 & HULLUCH Trench in A.196, also in conjunction with artillery shoot at 9 p.m. + 10.15 p.m. We fired 1000 rounds on A.26.a 17.09 & 1000 rounds on H.25.6.89.54 + 1000 rounds on H.26.c.38.74. Also the B.4.17 Battery in conjunction with artillery, we fired 2000 rounds on A.26.a.97.52 + H.26.c.63.08. In addition to this we fired from R.45 position, 1500 rounds on Track 1 Trench from H.14.c.65.00 to A.14.d.00.60, between Stroke + 11 may movement was observed there at Dusk: we fired 100 rounds at E.A.T. Co. following morning at 5 a.m. Our own planes were very active, flying low, strafing at enemy Trenches.	14

WAR DIARY
INTELLIGENCE SUMMARY

Army Form C. 2118.
137 M.G. Coy.
W.5.

Place	Date	Hour	Summary of Events and Information	Remarks and references to Appendices
MAZINGARBE	8/11/17		Ref. Sheet 36c NW 1/20000. Four Machine Guns at R.4.8 & HAY ALLEY SOUTH were laid to fire in conjunction with O.O. GERARD No. 89. If rocket was sent up, the guns were not opened for this, so were available for trench night firing. One gun at CURZON St. Battery fired 2000 rounds on DUMP in A.11.d.4 & H.13.b. Other guns, with our Anti-aircraft guns at R.4.5 & R.4.6, replied to enemy hostile at 3 E.A. which flew over our lines from WINGLES but E.A. came very low, shot when no guns fired, & at one time threw 'flare back & was on line WINGLES WATERTOWER & CRINNEY, were fought by our Lewis at 1.30 P.M - Bet 12 noon & 1 pm, some of the morning of the 5th. - Between FENDIN & WINGLES, 200 & 300 in totals of 80 -	
"	9/11/17		Our Battery in CURZON St. fired 1000 rounds on target in A.26.a, Gas was discharged in G.12.d at 11 P.M. Enemy retaliated from 11.15 P.M. to 11.45 P.M. by trench mortars of all kinds & 77 mm on our front & supporting line in G.12.d & G.18.c. The enemy gas shelled LONE TRACK & trench entrance at 1.10 P.M. on the morning of the 10, & got the same time heavily shelled the G.L.F.B.T. back areas & G.A.	1 O.R. to hospital Sec.R

WAR DIARY
INTELLIGENCE SUMMARY

Army Form C. 2118.

137th M.G. Coy
M.G.C.

Place	Date	Hour	Summary of Events and Information	Remarks and references to Appendices
MAZINGARBE	10.11.17		Ref Sheet 36 c N.W./20,000 In conjunction with artillery operations this evening, our Machine Guns carried out "shoots" from CURSON St. Battery, firing 6000 rounds on enemy strongpoints at A.14 a.10.32 & DUMP R.2 A.13.C.95.38, and from B.4/17 Battery at R.45a. We fired 712.5mm on targets as follows. Groups & trammings A.13.C.95.60 & Trench round A.8 a.10.20, also R.4.8 Gun fired 2000 rounds at H.8 a.10.20. The bursts of firing were, 7.30 p.m - 7 p.m - 8.30 p.m. 45.45 p.m. 12.15 midnight. The rates of fire being 2' intense & 3' normal for each occasion. The enemy first out retaliated. An E.A. came over our lines at 10.30 am on the 11th in Direction of WINGLES, our A.A. Gun at RUGHIES 2.57mm Rd. Another plane over at 11.15am very high, it faced a little run fired 50 rounds. The enemy M.G's been active firing artillery range shoots on enemy M.G. just NORTH of PUITS 13 fired some bursts into CURSON St. at 12.15 midnight at the orders of our Artillery rung Schools from 132 & 1208 c/5.71.	1 O.R. to Hospital
"	11.11.17		Our Battery at CURSON St. fired 1000 rounds on M.T. 7&13, after firing the NORTHERN Shaft & T.O.H. spent, and 12 hung MINNENWERFER, roused the enemy Probably it was retaliation for our own Slanting pests at 8.45 p.m. T.M. activity from 12 noon to 4 p.m the enemy shelled us with 5.0.77 m.m to G.18 a from HULLUCH at 3.30 p.m. 8.4.2 to G.18 C from WINGLES. He also put down a barrage on Hill 70 from 3.45 p.m to 4 p.m & continued shelling the hill at intervals until 5 p.m. S.H.	1 O.R. returned from Hospital

Army Form C. 2118.

WAR DIARY
or
INTELLIGENCE SUMMARY.

137th A.S. Coy.
No. 7.

(Erase heading not required.)

Instructions regarding War Diaries and Intelligence Summaries are contained in F. S. Regs., Part II. and the Staff Manual respectively. Title pages will be prepared in manuscript.

Place	Date	Hour	Summary of Events and Information	Remarks and references to Appendices
MAZINGARBE	12-11-17		Ref Sheet 36c N.W. 1/20,000. Our Battery at CURSON St. fired 3500 rounds in cooperation with operations by G.U.V. They also fired 1000 rounds per our M.G. at HAY ALLEY SOUTH, on HOBART Trench from 8.45 p.m. to 9 p.m. We fired from R.48, 250 rounds into POITS 13, at same after, there were a noise of falling corrugated sheets, at any rate, 6. Several aeroplanes came over our lines 7. There were between 15 & 20 heavy MINENWERFER off firing very light. About 12 midnight, between their near FROM FUGEN SHAFT, about 13 midnight, between 11 am & 12 noon on the 13th AM, the enemy sent 20 77 mm on 618a from BULLOCH WOOD. Enemy M.G.'s were very active all night. Left AM RESERVE LINE.	1 O.R. to hospital. 1 O.R. Evacuated.
"	13-11-17		at CURSON St. Battery we fired 1500 rounds into Mulloch & Battery at BAY 17. Firing round Lt POITS 13, one E.A. flew over our lines from direction of VERMELLES to Lt POITS 13, one E.A. flew over our lines from O.A. Gun at R.48, 1570 rounds into WINGLES at 2.35 pm, we fired from our M.G. 3 x 4 bursts & NORTHERN about 30 to 40 heavy MINENWERFER fell round SHAFT firing the latter part of the afternoon.	1 O.R. Reinforcement.

Army Form C. 2118.

137th M.G.Coy
No. 8.

WAR DIARY
or
INTELLIGENCE SUMMARY
(Erase heading not required.)

Place	Date	Hour	Summary of Events and Information	Remarks and references to Appendices
MAZINGARBE	14.11.17		Ref. Sheet 36C.N.W. 1/20.000 Our Machine Guns at R4 & 5 fired 500 rounds at School House in HULLOCH A.13.b.70-80. From 11.5 P.m. to 11.30 P.m. enemy retaliated for our Gas operation, by sending over 100 to 150 whizbangs & an occasional 4-2" shell, on our RESERVE LINE & FRONT LINE, POSEN & HAY ALLEY. Visibility for the Sky was very poor.	1 O.R. wounded in action 14th.
	15.11.17		Our Battery at CURZON St. fired 2000 rounds during the night on track at H.20.C-d., The Battery at BAY 17. fired 2000 between 6 P.m. & 12 midnight on dump & track at H.14.c. or 8.0. At 3.25 P.m. 1 E.A. came over from Lees direction & passed over our R.4 S.A.A position, he fired 300 rounds, good shooting with tracer bullets was observed also passing through the E.A, the same Gun also fired 600 rounds, at the lower "Y" a formation of 6 E.A. flying over HULLOCH they then flew SouthwarD, Our A.A. Gun at R.4.8 fired 1000 rounds at the same planes. An increase of hostile shelling is noticed on POSEN & VEADIN (?), the corner of BROADWAY & RESERVE LINE was shelled at 3.25 P.m. by about 20 whiz. bangs, A great deal of transport was heard from TRACK and drawn from direction of TUIS 13. specially East of Pit. A.H.	

WAR DIARY or **INTELLIGENCE SUMMARY**

Army Form C. 2118.

137th M.G. Coy
No. 9

Place	Date	Hour	Summary of Events and Information	Remarks and references to Appendices
			Ref Sheet. 36C N.W. 1/20,000	
MAZINGARBE.	16.11.17		From our R+S position we fired 1500 rounds on the road passing through Hulluch at H8C7.0.0 to H8d5.6.0 firing from 5:30 p.m. to 10 p.m. from 3 a.m. to 5 a.m. Farm R+S.A.A. Gun we fired 1500 rounds at I.E.A. coming from direction of WINGLES. At 4:15 p.m. enemy sent up, split red lights, from his front line, between Bois de Dix Huit & No BSS ALLEY, these lights were taken up at once by enemy's reserve line, & in a bout 4 minutes he brought down a barrage of 6" & 8" shells on front line of Hill 70, the Barrage lasted just one minute, during which about 50 shells were fired, Enemy M.G's were very quiet all night. S.H.	2 O.R. to Hospital. 2 O.R. reinforcements.
"	17.11.17		Our Battery at CURSON ST. fired 4000 rounds in conjunction with artillery shoot. At Bay 17 we also carried out harassing fire on to H21a 40-70 at an active Battery position, 1000 rounds being fired. She fired 1500 rounds from A.A. Sunset R+S Position. Also from R+S A.A. Gun firing 1750 rounds. Over A.A. Gun at CURSON ST. fired 750 RDs at the same A.A. gun. Over A.A. Gun at CURSON ST. fired 750 RDs at the same plane at 7 a.m. Downing the first Artillery + Machine Gun shoot.	1 O.R. to Base H.Q.P. 1 O.R. to Hospital

WAR DIARY
INTELLIGENCE SUMMARY

Army Form C. 2118.

137th M.G. Coy
No. 10.

Place	Date	Hour	Summary of Events and Information	Remarks and references to Appendices
MAZINGARBE	17-11-17		Ref Sheet 36 C N.W. 1/20000 The enemy sent up Split Green Light, 4 in about 3 minutes, bright Town & Three Barrage, on our front line from Hill 70 to TOSEN, when enemy appeared to realize it was only harassing fire, he sent up "Split red lights," which were reported back towards his artillery. Enemy shell fire then gradually died away, something heavy lasted about 15 minutes his retaliation was made for 2 ns & 3rd platoon. The day following at 1 pm he sent over a dozen whizz-bangs in the region of BROADWAY & RESERVE LINE junction. J.H.	
"	18-11-17		Our Battery at CURSON ST. fired 2000 rounds into HULLUCH MAIN R.S. & round SCHOOL HOUSE, We also fired 750 rounds from BAY 17, between dusk & 9 pm on Trench junction & Tramway at H.16.6.25-40, then relaid on S.O.S. lights zone 1700 rounds were fired from A.4.8 on at R.1.a.5, at 8 E.A. 15 feet kept them behind their own lines & very high, he also engaged them at CURSON ST firing 150 rounds. Our L.A.A. Gun at R.1.b.5 hit 1000 rounds between 9.30am & 10.30am at 10.15am, 3 white lights were fired from enemy front line at H.19.a.70.50, These were repeated & sent back to enemy artillery! they fired about 20 – 5.9 shells at junction of ESSEX LANE & REGENT LINE, shooting was poor. They were noted by searching for T.M. emplacement. J.H.	1 O.R. wounded

Army Form C. 2118.

WAR DIARY
or
INTELLIGENCE SUMMARY.

(Erase heading not required.)

137th M.G.Coy.
A.O. 11.

Place	Date	Hour	Summary of Events and Information	Remarks and references to Appendices
			Ref. Sheet 36c N.W. 1/20,000	
MAZINGARBE	19.11.17		At CURZON St. Battery we fired 2000 rounds, during the night on HICKS ALLEY & 1000 rounds. Through the morning mist, at hostile working parties & to there was a fair amount of aerial activity, we fired 1250 rounds from our 4.5" Gun at R4-6, between 2 & 4.30 p.m., at 2 F.A. they did not cross over from their lines, but kept trying to approach. We also fired 2500 rounds over from their lines, but kept trying to approach. We also fired 2500 rounds in the afternoon at an E.A. (ALBATROSS), evidently looking for T.M. emplacements. The same part of our line, for 2 days. This machine has patrolled the same part of our line, for 2 days. Enemy sent 6 rounds 4.5 - 9" on VENDIN ALLEY near RESERVE LINE at 12.45 p.m. on the 20th Nov:-	1 O.R. to Hospital. 1 O.R. from Hospital 8 O.R. Reinforcements.
"	20.11.17		Our Battery at Curzon St. fired 200 rounds on H.26.a, and in confirmation with raid by 11th Div., the same Battery fired 1000 rds. on H.26.a.34.18/10.20 minutes. Also Battery from Bay 17. fired 1500 rds. from 5.30 a.m. to 4 a.m., sweeping parapet of HULLUCH Trench from HICKS ALLEY to HINDOO, & in letter Battery in confirmation with raid fired 2500 rds. Sweeping HULLUCH Trench from HICKS to HONEY ALLEY. 2000 rds. 9 cartridge Guns at R4's emptying target at H.26.d.50.65 to H.26.d.90.45, at R4.8 we fired 1500 rds. going on explosive creeping barrage on k H.15.G.70.20 to H.25.G.82.27, H.25.G.97.38, k H.15.G & H.26a, for 45 After our artillery had bombarded enemy's trench in H.25.G & H.26a, for 45 minutes he then began to retaliate on front & Reserve line in response to GREEN LIGHT, from the shelled area. His parapet searched by night	

WAR DIARY
or
INTELLIGENCE SUMMARY.

Army Form C. 2118.

137th M.G. Coy.
No. 12.

Place	Date	Hour	Summary of Events and Information	Remarks and references to Appendices
MAZINGARBE	20.11.17	Ref. Sheet 36 c N.W. 1/5,000	Our BAY17 Guns, was pushed up & held. At 6.11 a.m. on the 2nd time, the artillery & M.G. fire, every sent up S.O.S. dawn rain, & rather suddenly brought down enemy barrage. His retaliation came down in RESERVE LINE, one shell dropping in the A.A. position at R.4.5, & burst in the trench there. The fire of BAY17 Battery is evidently Hulluch & Haisnes has evidently very effective, and the enemy M.G.'s are very active firing a raid, bullets dropping on the Reserve Trench. But the Trench they were endeavouring by this to harass, would 5 minutes after our Battery had ceased fire.	4 O.R. reinforcements
"	21.11.17		At CURSON St. our Battery fired 4000 Rds. in conjunction with Artillery harassing fire on HOBBS ALLEY & nr mean Trench from A25.c.9.6, 40 & A26.a.25.22 at 7.35 P.m. – 10.5 P.m. – 2 a.m. & 2.30 a.m. Bay 17 Battery fired 1500 rds. During the night on junction of HULLUCH & ST INDOO. Fired a 1000 rds from 2 M.G. & 2 Guns at BAY17 this morning at 6 a.m. & 3000 rds from our Left Sector Guns, owing to S.O.S. going up on A.1.11.79, firing at gun barrage asked dated for & open hour, supported by M.G. firing. Our artillery opened fire on ATTACK HIVE at 6.15 a.m. was continued firing until 7 a.m. Enemy fire died away at 6.30 a.m.	L.H.

WAR DIARY
or
INTELLIGENCE SUMMARY

Army Form C. 2118.

137# M.G. Coy
No. 13.

Ref. Sheet 36aNW. 1/20000

Place	Date	Hour	Summary of Events and Information	Remarks and references to Appendices
MAZINGARBE	22-11-17		We had orders on the 21st Nov. at 5.9/44, to carry out a harassing scheme from M.G's on specially selected, whose work is thus to begin on, "Targets" & Bridges over trenches constantly in use, the fire programme was carried as follows, H26c60.90 - A7c90.60 - A7a50.00 - G1269v.30 G1267v.35 on Batteries at Curson St. & B4y17 carried thout, firing 4000 rounds throughout the night, All our OLd Sn-RH5, we fired 150 rds at an EA flying over our line from 10.30 am to 11.00 a.m. that was a certain amount of movement in HERCULES Trench in the track behind, but not in Groups. J.H.	1 O.R. from hospital
"	23-11-17		In accordance with our M.G. "Night harassing programme, on specially selected targets, We fired from B4y17, R45 1500 Rds, from CURSON St 1000 Rds, & R117 - R48 1500 Rds. Total 4000. Targets were, Support work tracks, Dumps & Trench Cross used by Ration Parties, & enemy M.G's one from Hullvch & one from about A426a10.60. retaliated to our shortfiring the wire at night, sweeping RESERVE Trench at B4y17.	1 O.R. Yol hospital
"	24-11-17	2.30 p.m. the following day, enemy cult, 10% m.77	Opt Curson St Battery & Destruction to selected targets, result fired 1500. A7c9.0.60 - A7a50.00, at large about Turnwaetre was obtained coming from Aullvch, H7c9.0.60 - A7a50.00 R.S.P. Our 18 Pbny had been firing at that area just about H.14a at 2.30 p.m. R.S.P. At H7c 35.18 at 2.30 p.m. the following day, enemy cult, 10% m.77 mm. en #244 from Hullvat D.M.	1 O.R. from hospital

WAR DIARY
INTELLIGENCE SUMMARY

Army Form C. 2118.

137th M.G. Coy.
No. 14.

Place	Date	Hour	Summary of Events and Information	Remarks and references to Appendices
MAZINGARBE	25-11-17		Ref Sheet. 36c.N.W. 1/20000 In accordance with night harassing scheme on selected targets we fired from CURSON St 1250 R¹ds, from BA7/17 + R45- 1250, Total 2500 R¹ds. One E.A. (Aviatik), flew over our lines at 11.30 a.m. & circled round until 11-50 a.m. Our A.A. guns fired 2750 n¹ds; It then returned towards VENDIN-LE-VIEIL. One Albatross flew over towards PHILOSOPHE at a great height at 12.30 p.m. 15 hostile m our guns & fire, our RESERVE LINE was shelled this morning from 10.30 to 12 midday by about 50 to 60. - 77mm from guns in CITÉ ST ELIE - HULLUCH & Bois DES DAMES. Wt 11.30 A.M. m⁰ 25ᵉ - 12 w.h.3" Lamps were sent into TENTH AVENUE, the same number at 7 a.m. m⁰ 26 ¹ - about 20. 5. 5"₂ were fired at our batteries behind CURSON St. between 1.30pm + 2pm m 26 ᵗʰ U.K.	1.O.R. to hospital 1.O.R. to hospital
"	26-11-17		Our harassing fire from CURSON St- BA7/17 +R45, was directed against the following targets - H27a 60.30 - H20a 70.40 - H26c 60. 80 - H20a 05. Gov Minutes, total rounds 3750. One PUITS 13 our enemy M.G. was worrying our Infantry, we retaliated with our M.G. at R48, into PUITS 13, & the enemy Gun gave no more trouble, at 10.30 a.m. on the 27ᵗʰ the enemy put about 12 w.h.3 lamps on the RESERVE LINE of BROAD WAY from VENDIN-LE-VIEIL. O.K	1.O.R. to U.K. M.G. movement

WAR DIARY or INTELLIGENCE SUMMARY

Army Form C. 2118.

137 M.G. Coy - NO. 15

Place	Date	Hour	Summary of Events and Information	Remarks and references to Appendices
MATINGARBE	27.11.17		Ref. Sheet 36C N.W. 1/20000. From 3' Battery R.45 we carried out harassing fire on selected targets firing 1500 rds - A.W. gun at R.4.5 - CURSON St - V.R.+8. Fired 4.200 rds between 12.30p - 1p.m. on the 28th at an E.A. (Cavalry P.K.) which was very persistent. The enemy sent H.E. + Gas shells into area of VERMELLES - HULLUCH Rd. near RESERVE LINE between 6p.m. 9/12 midnight. About 6 of each at irregular intervals of the hour, shells were 4.2's. E.A.	
	28.11.17		Harassing fire carried out as per programme on special targets from CURSON St - R.4.8 - R.4.5 - Day 17 - Firing in all 2750 rds. We fired from A.A. Guns 4500 rds. being a great deal of aerial activity specially from 8am to 1pm. 5 E.A. were over our lines from 9.30 to 10.30 am. Gas was projected into CITE St ELIE at 10.30 pm, the enemy retaliated with his M.G's at once, also lights, split reds + greens - golden lights + golden rain were sent up, from his front line + repeated back his artillery, at 10.36 pm he dropped a barrage on front line, lifting to reserve at 11 P.m. E.A.	

WAR DIARY
INTELLIGENCE SUMMARY

Army Form C. 2118.

137th M.G.Coy
No: 16

Ref Sheet 36C N.W./20000

Place	Date	Hour	Summary of Events and Information	Remarks and references to Appendices
MAZINGARBE	29.11.17		At CURSONST. — Bay 17 & R+8 M.G. carried out the night harassing programme on special targets, firing in all 3500 rds. The aeroplane programme at 3 F.A. (approxtly), flying low over our lines from 1100 rds of 3 F.A. (approxtly), flying low over our lines from SOUTH to NORTH at 2 P.m., they only circled round for 5 minutes then flew sharply away in a NORTHerly direction, for an Artillery shoot in the afternoon. The enemy retaliated at 6 p.m. & bombarded huts & RESERVE KINGS, keeping it up until 5.20 am its morning MINNIES & HEAVIES were very fresh, we have very silent with Trench, aft our M.G. posn in at RMG six different enemy M.Gs swept the emplacement & all round that vicinity, an enemy dump was blown up in the direction of Pt 08 – SSE E at 5:45 p.m. N.A.	
"	30.11.17		Harassing fire was carried out by our M.G. at the targets at 12:15 p.m. to hut opposite enemy on HERCULES TRENCH firing 3000 rds. One selected targets, 12:15 p.m. to hut opposite enemy on HERCULES TRENCH firing 3000 rds. H.D.O.G. 40.80 was fired upon by our M.G. at RM7, firing 250 rds rapid at enemy, At 9–10 p.m. a very heavy shoot by enemy on our front & our left was commenced. The S.O.S. on our left went up, Red light, from Sussex instantly opened fire, from LEFT & RIGHT Sections, firing 12,250 rds. We enough to left S.O.S. went up again, we fired a further 12500 rds. About 5:45 am an M.W. bombarded our HILL 70, & our S.O.S. green light went up. Our guns instantly fired on aft. 500 rds on Rgt H SOS tracer.	1 O.R. from Hospital J.H

Army Form C. 2118.

137th US Coy
No. 17.

WAR DIARY
INTELLIGENCE SUMMARY.
(Erase heading not required.)

Place	Date	Hour	Summary of Events and Information	Remarks and references to Appendices
MAZINGARBE			Ref sheet 36 C N.W. 1/20000	
			Total reinforcements for the month. 15	
			Total Wounded 3	
			Sick to Hospital. 11	
			From Hospital. 6	
			To Base. 2	
			To Cadet School England 1	
			Returned after Evacuation. 1	
			Evacuated 1	

Leslie R.S. Nevins Lt.
137th U.S.
i.e. for O.E.
Nov. 30th 1917.

To H.Q.
137 Bde

Herewith War Diary of
137' M.G.Coy. for month of
December. 1917

Leslie R.G.Heina Lt.
O.C.
137' M.G.Coy

No. 137
MACHINE GUN
COMPANY.
No.
Date 1. 1. 18.

Army Form C. 2118.

WAR DIARY
INTELLIGENCE SUMMARY
(Erase heading not required.)

137th M.G.C
No: 1

Place	Date	Hour	Summary of Events and Information	Remarks and references to Appendices
MAZINGARBE	1-12-17		Ref Sheet 36 c N.W. 1/20,000 At CURSON SE Battery – Bay 17 – Ru 8-9 H7 was fire 2500 rds on special targets, much wood trench, d trench etc. Our U.A. Guns fired 900 rds at E.M. between 10 a.m. & 11 a.m. on the morning of the 2nd, d trench etc. Our M.G. stopped our RESERVE LINE firing 160 a/t rounds of the 12 M/C flying fairly high. Enemy shelled our RESERVE LINE firing 160 a/t rounds on the morning early 2nd. Th 5.9's. Our shell falling 5" from R.47 Gun. Knocking in Th trench, & Th 4 min. early 2nd. Th RESERVE Garrison emplacement, the right was such just a few yards failing between RESERVE Garrison. An E.M.G. occurred our Battery from about H13.45.5.2 during the night. D.H.	
~	2-12-17		Harassing programmes carried out from CURSON St. Bay 17 from 1500 rds. Firing for Keeping enemy wire open at H70.40 to H70.13.63, at intervals during the 24 hours. Patrols were not out at no time down, also on Sap to in our E.M.G. H.25.B.46.60, H15.D.38.03, firing 200 rds. Sound were fired at an E.M.G. emplacement at H19.6.90.60. Enemy guns previously causing a [?] [?] trouble, where fired 750 rds between 2.30 & 2.53 p.m. Enemy also used RESERVE LINE round R.45 with F.2. Sweeping & searching. WING SN 41 was heavily shelled with MINNIE's this evening at 5 p.m.	1.0 p.m. to Habrik.l. R.H.
~	3-12-17		Enemy known two or three light trips firing 2750 rds also on some gaps in wire at 40 [?]. Bekain 1150 p.m. & 1 u.S. R.45, R.45 fired 150 rds between 7.15 a.m. & 7.30 a.m. & 550 rds between 1.30 p.m. & 1. u.S.R.45, R.45 fired 150 rds. CURSON SE. During enemy was active in the air, many planes up.	R.H.

WAR DIARY
INTELLIGENCE SUMMARY

137th M.G. Coy
No. 2

Place	Date	Hour	Summary of Events and Information	Remarks and references to Appendices
MAZINGARBE	4.12.17	36 C N.W. 1/20000	The harassing fire took place from CURSON St. & BAY 17, rounds fired were 3000. We also have gap in wire to keep them at H.7.c.13.63 & vicinity, rounds fired 1600. The work being done in conjunction with mines from 135, 136, 138, as the movement of Working Parties. The enemy aeroplanes were very active during the morning & afternoon, we had 1 O.P. from our A.A. Guns 3250 rds. It also had its observation balloons up, at dawn four Machines on Left this morning for the unteaching at 6.45. Now enemy opened harassing fire from our Left which lasted for 5 or 10 minutes, our gun at H.9.a.71.65. NORTH, fired 250 rds. J.H.R.	1 O.R. at down for hospital
—	5.12.17		We fired on selected targets from our two Battery positions 2000 rds. for keeping gap in wire open 2000 rds. Our A.A. Guns fired 300 rds at E.A. intensely in the afternoon. The tracer bullets appeared to be going right into the E.A. blindingly its last strike a vital part, as the machine turned & dived over Wingles & Chassé — the night was quiet, only a promenarm & telling behind RESERVE LINE. J.H.R.	
—	6.12.17		For harassing fire on speis Q (target), we fired 2000 rds, for keeping gap open in wire 1000 rds. We also fired this morning being misty, on BENIFONTAINE TRACK & wires at H.14.6; Our A.A. Sund. at CURSON St. & R&B, assisted 1 R.R.C. in bringing down 1 E.A. on the morning of 7.5. The E.A. was an ALBATROSS (D.III) Single Seater flying towards PHILOSOPHE, he fired 400 rds. at 8.10.20 a.m. It came down at G.11.a. an enemy TRENCH Mortar dump about H.19.d.40.79, was lit at 11.30 a.m. causing explosion J.H.	

WAR DIARY
INTELLIGENCE SUMMARY

Army Form C. 2118.

137th M.G. Coy.
No. 3

Place	Date	Hour	Summary of Events and Information	Remarks and references to Appendices
MAZINGARBE	7-12-17		Ref. Sheet 36 c N.W. 1/20000	
			For harassing fire on selected targets, rounds fired 1500, & in conjunction with our left Brigade, for keeping Sap open 3950; from our W & 4 Guns we fired 250 rds. at 3 E.A. over our lines at 2130 p.m.	1 Officer transferred to 139 Bde. 1 Officer transferred to this Coy.
~	8-12-17		CURSON ST. Battery 1 & 47 fired 200 rds, for selected targets, & in keeping Sap open 1250, & being misty, in the morning by the 4th Gun we fired 500 rds. to HERCULES TRACK, H148 + d. – We fired 750 rds. from R148, a 4-8 gun at 3 E.A. over our lines from 3 p.m. to 3.30 p.m. probably observing for enemy batteries, to which were also telling tunnel exits. Enemy Artillery & Trench Mortars very active this morning on our left Sector, RESERVE FRONT LINES were shelled for 10 minutes at 10.45 a.m. HAY ALLEY was also shelled with 5.9+.	1 O.R. to Hospital
~	9-12-17		Our Guns fired 1750 rds. for harassing fire, & 1000 rds. for keeping Sap open in zones, one E.A. crossed our lines from CITE St. ELIE & returned over HULLUCH at 10 a.m. 500 rounds were fired, 2 E.A. crossed our lines between 8 a.m. & 7.30 a.m. 750 rds. were fired, our Heavy Artillery exploded a very large dump a but H19280 40 at Major Sutaliens quiet on our front.	1 O.R. to Hospital 1 O.R. to Hospital
~	10-12-17		Our Battery Guns kept harassing fire on his left flank, firing 1500 rds. upon harassing fire, on selected targets, 1000 rds. From Bay 17 we fired 250 rds. on HULLUCH March, being a misty morning our 4 gun turned track 1 E.A. which tried to cross our lines near HULLUCH we fired 250 rds. Enemy quiet over about 30. H 268, W. RESERVE LINE in G24 & d fired 11 a.m. to 12 noon.	1 Officer to U.K. 1 Officer Reinforcement

WAR DIARY / INTELLIGENCE SUMMARY

Army Form C. 2118.

137th U.S. Coy.
No. 4

Place	Date	Hour	Summary of Events and Information	Remarks and references to Appendices
MAZINGARBE	11-12-17	36C N.W. 1/20000	In conjunction with the 139th L.T. M.Bty raid on our left, twelve of our guns took part in firing on flanks of raid, the Battery in CARSON St. fired for the Dummy Raid, from zero − 8 to zero + 1, firing 18,000 rds. Crossroads & Approaches at 8 of guns fired for the Raid Proper, firing 26,750 rds, from zero + 3 to zero + 10, all sweeping Rapid. Zero time was 3.40 p.m. Also from certain guns we fired short bursts throughout the night, harassing fire on selected targets, in & around BULLOCK & vicinity of raid. Less E.A. M.G. on our lines from 8.30 a.m. to 9 a.m., he fired 3 S.O.S. from R.V.S. 14.30 p.m. heavy but some gas shells on HAY DUMP at 5.30 p.m. subject. Note stations for the Raid. (Attempts for our M.G. fire for rifles. Sis over b. 271. A.L.	
	12-12-17		Harassing fire carried out on selected Targets, rounds fired 1800. At 9.50 p.m. during heavy enemy bombardment on our left, our guns fired on their LEFT S.O.S. again at 3.25 a.m. rds. 12000. Between 3-15 p.m. – 4.30 p.m. 7 E.A. flew over our lines, our guns fired 1750 rds. E.A. Aeroplane dropped bombs on RESERVE LINE & TENTH AVENUE bet: 8.30 & 9.30 a.m. RESERVE LINE was shelled at 12-45 a.m. with Gas Shells also TOSCH QUARRY Dumps, 4.30 & 2 A.M. LONE TRENCH at H.W. J.A.	

WAR DIARY
INTELLIGENCE SUMMARY.
(Erase heading not required.)

Army Form C. 2118.

137th M.G. Coy.
No. 35.

Place	Date	Hour	Summary of Events and Information	Remarks and references to Appendices
MAZINGARBE	13/12/17		We fired 36 ● N.W./9,000. Harassing fire on selected targets, & R.45 fired 250 rds on H 8a 30-10. Situated Quiet.	We fired 2750 rds. Harassing fire on selected targets, & R.45 fired 250 L.H.
"	14/12/17		The usual night harassing programme was carried out, firing 3000 rds. One E.A. flew over our lines from BOIS DES DAMES, Dir cd 8am at R.45 point 750 rds. It then turned round back in the same direction, about 2.50 a.m. yesterday, flew in at three, and is very high, where sent up, from the enemy front line, & artillery was brought to bear, on our front & second lines, between HAY ALLEY & BROADWAY, this lasted until 3.30 p.m.; The enemy shelled RESERVE LINE at 12.30 p.m. today with 4.2"&, 9.77 hows.	L.H.
"	15/12/17		We fired 2500 rds on selected targets. He fired 10 rds at a E.A. turning between 7.15 a.m. & 5.30 a.m. ——; Some 5' T.M. & T.M's fell round our emplacement at HAY ALLEY South between 2 p.m. & 3.30 p.m. Damaging it slightly. Being practically blown in.	2 O.R. wounded. L.H.
"	16/12/17		In accordance with 137th Bde. Memo c/176, we fired on Tracks & roads NORTH of H.13 & H.14 Central, also distr. 4500 expected 6th BAVARIAN Div. Relief. E.M. Cos very active during the night. Sniping RESERVE TRENCH.	1 O.R. to Hospital L.H.

Army Form C. 2118.

M. G. Coy
137th Inf. Bde. 6

WAR DIARY
INTELLIGENCE SUMMARY
(Erase heading not required.)

Instructions regarding War Diaries and Intelligence Summaries are contained in F. S. Regs., Part II. and the Staff Manual respectively. Title pages will be prepared in manuscript. Ref. Sheet.

Place	Date	Hour	Summary of Events and Information	Remarks and references to Appendices
MAZINGARBE	17-12-17	36c.N.W. 1/20000	In accordance with expected relief, we continued with firing on road tracks & roads, also vicinity of HULLUCH, rounds fired 4750. At 8 a.m. on the 18th there was 1 Al BATT ROSS SCOUT patrolling between HULLUCH & BOIS HUGO. We fired 350 rounds. The E.M.G.N. were not so active as on previous night, enemy shelled our front line about POSEN at 2 a.m., with a few lonely bomps at 4.20 A.M.	
"	18-12-17		Firing continued on targets likely to be used by enemy, road tracks & bombing planes over at irregular intervals during afternoon, flying high. Our A.A. Guns fired 1350 rds., the night was quiet.	
"	19-12-17		Our Guns fired 12,500 rds. in vicinity of HULLUCH & SCHOOL HOUSE, 4500 on HULLUCH Trench, at "STAND TO" this morning being very misty. At 2pm 5 ALBATROSS came over our lines, & 3 P.M 2 E.A's came over, at 3 P.M. 3 albatros we fired 500 rds. The situation is quiet very hazy fog, guns mounted all day	
"	20-12-17		Harassing fire carried out on tracks roads, rds. fired 8750. no aerial activity owing to thick fog, night very quiet.	
"	21-12-17		Harassing fire on selected targets rds. fired 3500, a great deal of aerial activity, our A.A. guns fired 700 rds. patrolling of 2", 4 & 5 A, also 6 E. Bothers up between 11am & 1.20pm. M.22 greatest activity. 1 E.A. flying near the Quadrilateral, very persistent. Reserve line shelled near R.17, rds 30.77mm. Also Mrs O.P. at Nay ALLEY SOUTH. He shelled with 77 m.m., Q.2. was in front of CURSON ST. BATTERY.	

WAR DIARY

INTELLIGENCE SUMMARY
(Erase heading not required.)

Army Form C. 2118.

137th M.G.C.
M.O. 1

Place	Date	Hour	Summary of Events and Information	Remarks and references to Appendices
MAZINGARBE	22·12·17		Ref. Sheet 36cNW 1/20000. Our Guns fired on enemy Trench defences during the night. Several H.E.A. were fired on by our M.G. guns at 4 p.m. 22nd, 4 S.E.A. on the 23rd at 2.30 p.m., identified two a high clock nearest near R47 was shelled thr. morning of the 23rd. L.77 also O.P. at Hay Alley. Sall. Meeting attended by 2.0.-Thirty, a Military Band was heard in rear of Haillucourt. at BENIFONTAINE, at midday with 232. D.A.	
"	23·12·17		Usual harassing fire on tracks & roads, from CURZON st.—BAY 17—1847—p.8 and 3500. 1 E.A. over LOOS at 3 p.m. Enemy artillery shelled RESERVE LINE between HAY ALLEY & ESSEX LANE in the afternoon, between 3·4 p.m. with 4·2's D.H.	1 O.R. to Hospital
—	24·12·17		Trench mortars were engaged during the night, one unit fired 5500, the next one 500 at 9 p.m. enemy did not retaliate for 20 minutes after, he then shelled HULLUCH-VERMELLES Rd. & VENDIN ALLEY, he also shelled round our gun positions at HAY ALLEY with 4·2's. Military Band again heard in direction of DOUVRIN. D.H.	1 O.R. Reinforcement
—	25·12·17		For Xmas we carried out special programme, from 6.45 p.m. throughout the night, engaging the enemys H.Q's—Trench Junctions, Hulluch Trench, E.M.G. & Pheaps, Supposed Dugouts, all tracks & roads, also aerial attention being paid to Hulluch trench, R.O.V. School, &c. Guns fired 18,000 rounds, our Stokes gun fired on an ALBATROSS scout at 1.30 p.m. firing 5 rounds, a train was seen at back of WINGLES from 7.30 a.m. seen on the 26th. Drum Band, single & with orchestra, apparently from a bagat at 10 p.m. Considerable shelling of RESERVE LINE between HAY ALLEY & BUNRADY. L.P.H.	

WAR DIARY

INTELLIGENCE SUMMARY.

Army Form C. 2118.

137W Inf. Bn
No. 8

Place	Date	Hour	Summary of Events and Information	Remarks and references to Appendices
MILINCOURT R.1.19		Ref Sheet 36 C.N.W. 1/20000	Our guns carried out harrassing fire on tracks & roads during the night firing 2500 rounds. At 7.15 am 2 EA's circled over Hulluch at 3.30 am our Lewis gun fired 65 rds. at 7.30 am 2 E.A's at 375 + 7 Serrens were seen by an M.G. team at R45. In reply our M.G. at R26.20.80 fired at there 4 one fired at 4-5 were seen to drop, 4 were journeyed they were at tree level. A few minutes later one E.A. quite high took up a position . . . . [illegible] a few minutes later our M.G fired 100 rounds at a C BOMBA M.V Tunnel entrance between 10-11am. 12.30 pm were fired at G. BOMBA M.V Tunnel entrance. There was
	27.12.17		Continued harassing fire on tracks & roads. Litering more shells, mostly a good deal of aerial activity, one fired 508 6 enemy formating shell at 9.45 am 3 have fixed or hostile gun pit Kemmalmar, 11 M.G. guns fired 2500 rds. Enemy sent over about 6.080 shells "MUSTARD" round POSEN DUMP & FIRM'H AVENUE, he also shelled in front of SHAFFIELD RESERVE LINE most of the evening, he sent over RMM gasoline + tear + tears and gun at R48. Making it very uncomfortable. Fine during the evening. H.A.	10.R. Room SHAFFIELD
	28.12.17		We fired 2500 rds. on tracks & Huts. During night, at 6 am 2 EA's came low over our lines from direction of HULLUCH WOOD, at 8 am 1 Aviatic Buick & other forms line 7. L & V S.A. Any C.R.A. sent field 2750 rds. During last most GAS SHELLS on GENIGH AVENUE, ER 3 gons & 9 am on 2S.F. MUSTARD GAS. D.H.	

Army Form C. 2118.

137th M.G.C.

NO. 9

WAR DIARY

INTELLIGENCE SUMMARY.

(Erase heading not required.)

Place	Date	Hour	Summary of Events and Information	Remarks and references to Appendices
MAINGARDE.	25-12-17		Ref Sheet. 36C.N.W. 1/20,000. He fired 3000 M.G. on selected traps during night. Enemy dropped some about 9 p.m. in hut of RESERVE LINE during evening. Later were Gas shells on our Right sector at 12 midnight, at 6 a.m. a shot and shell, similar to our usage of new Gas projector.	
	30-12-17		He fired 20,000 rounds harassing fire. A few Gas shells again fell at Quarry.	1 O.R. otherwise to Hospital.
			He fired 20,000 rounds, robot Zos to Liftenup near R44 position at 5.30 p.m. indiscriminate firing by enemy.	L.H.
	31-12-17		Our usual program carried out, firing 30,000 rds. on tracks & roads at 10.20 a.m. 11 a.m. 1.45 p.m. 4.30 p.m. E.A's over, dropped bomb at 5 a.m. this morning. Enemy put down a Barrage on RESERVE LINE at 5 a.m. with 4.2/5.9 & 7 M/m, this quieted down at 5.45 a.m. also bombarded m/hospital LEFT, all guns were ready & all teams, Starting to hit 2nd L.O.O.L. of fire but top He sheen no hit fairly heavily at some times, he also received vicious at 10.45 mins firing rifles on P.3 Snipers R46 & R49 with M.G. fire.	1 O.R. to Hospital L.H.

Leslie R.S. Plewitt
for O.C. 137th M.G.C.

WAR DIARY
INTELLIGENCE SUMMARY

Army Form C. 2118.

137th T.M.B.C. No. 1

Place	Date	Hour	Summary of Events and Information	Remarks and references to Appendices
MAZINGARBE	1-1-18	36 C.N.W. 1/20,000 Ref Sheet	At 8 p.m. this evening the S.O.S. went up on our Right, a U.S. gun at C.22.B.41.35 from D.24.17 & D.H.9. immediately opened fire. Before the S.O.S. signal dropped firing rapid. 14,750 rounds all from duck & 7 A.M. we fired 500 rds on enemy's S.P. Aeroplane hostile were up during the morning between 10.10 a.m. & 11.30 a.m. in direction of H.11 & H.17.D. In alarm of Trench mortar fire, one E.A. was brought down in flames at 11.10 a.m. A cracked with own lines. One M.G. fire at another firing rapid at the E.A. at the E.A. Tracer bullets appeared to be going straight into it. Normal fire. During morning 300, at 3pm & 3.30pm flares were behind WINGLES, from 1am & 2.30am. heavy transport at LULU & PUITS 13, Fort HULLUCH & OPPY RO	1 O.R. from Hospital
"	2-1-18		Again this morning in response to S.O.S. signal on our left B.G.s Bde. our guns opened at 9.30 Nine Batt'y S.O.S. Barrage lasting firing 12,500 rds & heavy Enemy convoys moving 9 & 7 p.m. we fired 1000 & checking fire 1500, between 8 p.m. & 10 p.m. on E.A.'s Transport on road in HULLUCH-LOOS area.	1 O.R. to Hospital
"	3-1-18		Notified 3500 Rds in Tracks & roads from direction of Carvin. One smith fabricated between HULLUCH Hill 70 & 1 km.N.E. & N.E. of San Fin 1 S card, & 7 S.O.R. at another road Heavy E.A. A Battery in front of VERDUN fired about 20-77 Rds on RESERVE LINE & 0.P.M. I.D.R	
"	4-1-18		12.30 p.m. 5 E.A. flew over from direction of VERDIN at fair at RESERVE LINE on upper 3500 Rds were fired at them by M/G & A.A. fire, 30 & 30 rds from T.M fell near May & Ley Nos & Soap & at 3 p.m. a train with wounded trips at Midnight, heavy Transport on HULLUCH-BENIFONTAINE Rd as intended throughout the night.	to Bde and underage (S.B.D. 1383)

Ref C4 M24

WAR DIARY

INTELLIGENCE SUMMARY

137th M.S.C.
No. 2

Army Form C. 2118.

Place	Date	Hour	Summary of Events and Information	Remarks and references to Appendices
MARINGARBE	5-1-18	Refsheet 36 C N.W. 1/20000	Harassing programme continued. 250 rds being fired on all proposed intersections. E.A. were over during the afternoon between 2 p.m. & 3.15 p.m. he fired 200 rds. 2D, of the 1st F.A. at 3 p.m., it was afterwards observed to descend near VENDIN. He fired a further 300 rds at 2 o'clock also fairly high towards HULLUCH.	1 O.R. to Hospital
	6-1-18		Harassing fire 2500 rounds on tracks & roads, also proposed area, + 357 rds at F.A. at 3 p.m., All Quiet very quiet during night	1 O.R. to Hospital 2/Lt ...
	7-1-18		150 rds neutralised intermittent fire, 6 E.A. out of Pt. 2 albatros flew near VENDIN very high, but by ??? about 30-40 rds (neutralised) near POSEN DUMP.	Lt. ...
	8-1-18		Harassing fire, 2000 rds, tracks & roads, at 10.30 a.m. 6 E.A. kept over our lines at 12 noon, 1 E.A. high over our lines, rounds fired 800, 6 E.A. 4-4.10 p.m. separating from No RFH of Bois Hugo, at 12.30 p.m. enemy shelled RESERVE LINE around R47 ??? 77 ??? + 4.2", Situation Quiet.	L.T.
	9-1-18		Our Guns fired 4000 rds on to enemy tracks, roads & trenches, from 9.30 am to 11.30am, our 1 A.A. Guns fired 3750 rds at 3 E.A's, enemy M.G's active on R47- respectively L/N 10th Hospital	1 O.R.
	10-1-18		He fired 2000 rds. harassing fire on trenches, roads etc, one E.A. fairly high he fired 10 rds fired about 30 ??? 240 to 10th AVENUE between 8.15pm + 9.45 pm, 46 & 10.30 to 11.45 p.m. POSEN ???	
	11-1-18		Harassing fire 3000 rds. In supp. of Raid by Canadian Batt. Two Guns fired on trenches NORTH OF HOBBS Alley, at 2.10 a.m., being zeroshout rounds fired 500, from 9 a.m. to noon 1800 rds, on 35 A patrolling our lines, at 2.40 am enemy retaliated on RESERVE LINE with 4-9" + 77mm whizz to Hospital T.M's for about 20 minutes, at Zero he sent up double green very lights.	1 O.R. Lt.

WAR DIARY
INTELLIGENCE SUMMARY

Army Form C. 2118.

137th I/C
No 3

Place	Date	Hour	Summary of Events and Information	Remarks and references to Appendices
MAZINGARBE	12-1-18		Usual harassing programme carried out, and to field wns. There was a great deal of aerial activity, consisting of 12 aeroplanes, 20 being up at the same time, most of them flying high. One S.A. Gun fired 850 rnds, also 16 Balloons up during morning. 6 of the field work p.m. 8 a.m. to 2 p.m. Enemy sent over 77 hvys rnds on our front. Sec. at R.H. 9.1. at 9 p.m. lamp signalling from MILMA of HULLUCH.	I.O.R. To Hospital R.H.
"	13-1-18		Arr carried out harassing fire on roads & tracks firing 2000 rnds. An enemy T.M. was seen firing at "Stand to" at about H.13.d.00.10. He will possibly firing R.H.Q. 6183	To Hospital No. 2
"	14-1-18		We fired 1500 rds. in ADHOCK Trench, between HINDOO & HICKS ALLEY, & 800 rds. in assisting the CANADIAN Raid. Keeping down M.G. fire at junction of HULLUCH Trench & HONEY ALLEY, at junction of HORSEAHEY, Aerial, at 3:30 p.m. 1 ALBATROSS over our lines, two S.A.Gun fired 250 rds. A number of green lights were sent up from enemy lines on our front, during the CANADIAN Raid. The night was fairly quiet, but for a few H.V.s, & large RESERVE LINE, between RH.5 & IRMA'S WAY, & about 5500 more in front of R.H.6.	2 O.R. to Hospital I.R.
"	15-1-18		Harassing fire on Enemy roads firing 1750 rds, weather very bad and aerial activity. Train seen proceeding NORTH from WINGLES presumably returning at 11 a.m., situation NORMAL	I.H.

WAR DIARY
INTELLIGENCE SUMMARY.
(Erase heading not required.)

Army Form C. 2118.

137th M.G.C.
No. 4.

Place	Date	Hour	Summary of Events and Information	Remarks and references to Appendices
MALINGARBE. N.W. 1/20,000	16.1.18		Refsheet 36C N.W. 1/20,000 In conjunction with Artillery harassing programme, our CURZON ST Battery fired as follows, 1000 rds. on junction of HIVE & HULLUCH Trench; 1000 " on Trench Junct at I. Flag Head; 1000 " on HULLUCH Trench between HINDOO & HICKS ALLEYS; 1000 " on HULLUCH Trench between HINDOO & HICKS ALLEYS.	
"	17.1.18		We also fired 250 rds. at "Stand to" this morning, as the track was used outside the trench at HIVE ALLEY. No aerial activity. Enemy M.G's very active during the night, particularly between "Stand to" "Stand to" this morning, otherwise night was very quiet. We carried out harassing fire on Railway he held HINDOO ALLEY & H.20.a, which appears to be greatly used, firing during the night 1500 rds. also 500 rds. at "Stand to" on H. 9. c. 50-99 movement being observed near the Hospital. We fired 1250 rds. at one E.A. over our lines from 10.20 am to 11 am; Hill 70 & HULLUCH WOOD, reoccupied 200, Prisoners. Our Albatros patrolling between Hill 70 & HULLUCH WOOD. M.G's active during night.	1 O.R. from Hospital. 1 O.R. Evacuated. J.A.
"	18.1.18		Harassing fire, loss on useful targets, Railways & tracks etc. Between 10 am & 1 pm E.A.s patrolling our lines, our Guns fired 1870 rds. a little bombing from Hospital was heard on our Right about midnight, otherwise night was quiet. Enemy M.G's were active again.	10 P. 1 O.R. 1 O.R. Reinforcement

WAR DIARY
INTELLIGENCE SUMMARY

137th M.G.C.
No. 5

Army Form C. 2118.

Place	Date	Hour	Summary of Events and Information	Remarks and references to Appendices
MAZINGARBE	19.1.18		We carried out our usual harassing fire during the night, firing 2500 rounds on enemy night Railway, trenches, & roads, At 2.30 p.m. 5 ALBATROSS patrolled our lines, At 2.30 p.m. A.A. Guns fired 1500 rounds. At 3 p.m. 15 ALBATROSS Patrolled our Lines, but very high, out of our M.G. range. Enemy did a little indiscriminate shelling with 5.9's round TO-BEN. Vicinity.	1 O.R. from Hospital. 1 O.R. to Hospital.
"	20.1.18		1500 rounds harassing fire on tracks etc. Also 250 rounds anti-aircraft. Eight E.A. were patrolling enemy's lines at 4.15 p.m. but flying very high.	
"	21.1.18		1000 rounds harassing fire on selected targets. Aerial activity experienced between 9 a.m. and noon, and in all 1,350 rounds were fired.	
"	22.1.18		"S" Battery fired 1000 rounds with HIVE ALLEY between 5 and 9 p.m. 300 rounds were fired at E.A. The enemy put down a heavy barrage on CITE ST. AUGUSTE front at 5.20 p.m.	
"	23.1.18		At STUNTS 100 rounds was fired on enemy party seen entering HIVE ALLEY. In the evening 1000 rounds were fired on engaged obstacles at H20 A 85.30. Also 550 rounds were fired at 2 AEROPLANES Seen over our lines between 8.45 a.m. and 11.15 a.m.	
"	24.1.18		Harassing fire 2000 rounds on Railways and Dumps. Conditions unfavourable to aerial activity. Exhaustion Party.	
"	25.1.18		Company relieved in 12 guns by No. 33 M.G. Company, and in 2 guns by No. 32 Company. Company marched to rest billets at VENDIN-LEZ-BETHUNE. Enemy planes dropped bombs on BETHUNE.	
VENDIN	26.1.18 27.1.18		Company bathed and inspected. Guns and Gunmaterial cleaned, overhauled, and checked.	

Army Form C. 2118.

WAR DIARY

INTELLIGENCE SUMMARY. 137 M.G.Coy No 6

(Erase heading not required.)

Instructions regarding War Diaries and Intelligence Summaries are contained in F. S. Regs., Part II. and the Staff Manual respectively. Title pages will be prepared in manuscript.

Place	Date	Hour	Summary of Events and Information	Remarks and references to Appendices
			Ref. map 36 B.	
PENDIN	28.1.18		Elementary Training: Squad Drill, Arm Drill, Gun Drill. E 8 d central.	
	29.1.18			
	30.1.18			
	31.1.18			

46 Bn M.G Corps
Vol I

WAR DIARY

OF

137th MACHINE GUN COY.

FEBRUARY 1918.

Confidential
Secret.

WAR DIARY
INTELLIGENCE SUMMARY

Army Form C. 2118.

137 Machine Gun Company
Sheet 2

LENS 11 / BEAUMETZ-LEZ-AIRE & HAZEBROUCK 5A

Place	Date	Hour	Summary of Events and Information	Remarks and references to Appendices
	Feb.15	10 a.m	Farewell Address by Brigadier General Cunningham.	
			Company moved to new billets. 11.30 a.m. Route March from EQUIRRE through LISBOURG to	
			BEAUMETZ-LEZ-AIRE. Company now under D.M.G.O. for Training.	RP
BEAUMETZ-LEZ-AIRE.	Feb.16		C.O.'s Inspection. Cleaning Guns and gun limbers. Pay Parade.	RP
	Feb.17		Church Parade.	RP
	Feb.18		Training with limbers. 1 Section on Range (Divisional Musketry)	RP
	Feb.19		Company Drill, mounted. Barrage Drill. 1 Section on Range -	RP
	Feb.20		Gun Drill with limbers and pack animals, practical Transport from limber to packsaddles. Lectures on Parts of Harness.	RP
			1 Section on Range. Barrage Drill. Grouping Section on Range (Musketry). 2 Sections on M.G. Range.	RP
	Feb.21		Lectures on Barrage. Barrage Drill. 2 Section on M.G. Range.	RP
	Feb.22		Route March to Baths at LISBOURG. 3 Reinforcements from Base.	RP
	Feb.23		Transport and remainder of Company on Musketry Range. Pay Parade.	RP
			C.O.'s Inspection. Cleaning Guns and gun limbers.	RP
	Feb.24		Church Parade.	RP
	Feb.25		Company Parade under Subaltern for Officers. Box Respirator Drill. Testing of all Box Respirators. Lachrymatory.	RP
	Feb.26		Company Drill, dismounted. Judging Distances.	
			Address by Lt. Col. Hewett, commanding Divisional M.G. Batt. Lecture by Col. Holder on "Sickles stop".	
	Feb.27		Barrage Drill. Details on Range. Instruction of Company to Seaton by 1/1st N.M. Field Ambulance.	RP
Feb.28			to O.C. 137 Machine Gun Company

Army Form C. 2118.

WAR DIARY
or
INTELLIGENCE SUMMARY.
(Erase heading not required.)

137 Machine Gun Company

Army Corps: HAZEBROUCK
5A / 1/100,000
& LENS II / 1/40,000

Sheet 1.

Instructions regarding War Diaries and Intelligence Summaries are contained in F.S. Regs., Part II. and the Staff Manual respectively. Title pages will be prepared in manuscript.

Place	Date	Hour	Summary of Events and Information	Remarks and references to Appendices
VENDIN-LEZ-BETHUNE			Company in Rest Billets.	
	Feb. 1st 1918		} First stage of training. Squad Drill, Elementary Gun Drill, Physical Training	
	Feb. 2nd			R.
	Feb. 3rd		Church Parade. Baths.	R.P.
	Feb. 4		Route March — ANNEZIN, LABEUVRIERE, LAPUGNOY, FOUQUEREUIL, & back to VENDIN	R.P.
	Feb. 5		Company Drill	R.P.
	Feb. 6		46th Divisional Musketry Course. 1 Section on Range. Remainder, Company & Barrack Drill	R.P.
	Feb. 7		Route March in full marching order — CHOCQUES, GONNEHEM, OBLINGHEM, HINGES, BETHUNE, & back VENDIN.	R.P.
	Feb. 8		C.O.'s Inspection. Packing Limbers.	R.P.
	Feb. 9		46th Division moves further back. Two Day's' tactical scheme. Route March via ANNEZIN, LABEUVRIERE, LAPUGNOY, MARLES, LOTINGHEM, BURBURE, to HURIONVILLE. Inspection of 137th Inf. Brigade on march at LOTINGHEM by 1 Corps and 46th Division Commanders.	
HURIONVILLE	Feb. 10		Continuation of Brigade march. Through BELLERY, FONTAINE-LES-HERMANS, FONTAINE-LES-BOULANS, HEUCHIN, to EQUIRRE.	R.P.
EQUIRRE	Feb. 11		Company Baths and Inspection.	R.P.
	Feb. 12		} Resumed Training. Squad & Arms Drill. Company Drill. Barrack Drill.	R.P.
	Feb. 13			R.P.
	Feb. 14			R.P.

www.ingramcontent.com/pod-product-compliance
Lightning Source LLC
Chambersburg PA
CBHW081530160426
43191CB00011B/1729